~1988~

Donna –
Thanks for
being such a
special friend!
Love,
Donna

Up to
heaven
and
down to
earth

Up to heaven and down to earth

Fay Angus

A Division of G/L Publications
Glendale, California, U.S.A.

The Scripture quotations in *Up to Heaven and Down
to Earth* are from the *Authorized King James Version.*

© Copyright 1977 by G/L Publications
All rights reserved
Printed in U.S.A.

Published by
Regal Books Division, G/L Publications
Glendale, California 91209, U.S.A.

Library of Congress Catalog Card No. 76-29890
ISBN 0-8307-0472-8

To Ann and Ian, with love

Other good Regal reading by Fay Angus
Between Your Status and Your Quo

Contents

Introduction

The British like to be introduced. Indeed it is possible for generations of Englishmen to stare coldly through generations of other Englishmen without ever being on speaking terms, merely through the lack of a proper introduction. The Colonial British are even more so, and being a product of this now endangered species I was reared under the strict formal code of never speaking to a stranger unless we had been introduced.

If God Himself had knocked on our door and said "How nice to see you, Fay," I'm sure my rather tart reply would have been, "I say there, Sir, we haven't been introduced."

Fortunately for me, in due time I was introduced to God, through the auspices of His Son, Jesus Christ, who soon became my Lord and Saviour. I have been on very

10

intimate speaking terms with Him ever since. Even more fortunately for me, God Himself was introduced to me through the very same auspices and is on equally intimate speaking terms with me, most frequently speaking intimately through His Holy Writ.

Now embarking on a writ of my own, it is my most earnest desire to be on thoroughly good, and perhaps even intimate, speaking terms with my readers. Hence the necessity of this introduction.

In the background, my *paternal* grandfather was sent out to China from Australia in 1892 by the China Inland Mission. In the same era, not to be outdone, my *maternal* grandfather set out from England to explore the excitement of the Orient on his own initiative. He ended up commanding a large garrison in the interior of China training Chinese Army Officers—one grandfather being with the CIM, the other being with the CAO, and fortunately, neither being with the CIA!

These facts validate the Chinese heritage of both my mother and my father who—though thoroughly British —were born, educated, met and married in China. While my parents were on a short furlough to visit their folks in Brisbane, Australia, I made an appearance; born, I'm told, in a kangaroo's pocket. Which no doubt accounts for my somewhat jumpy disposition and the fact that "Waltzing Matilda" is one of my favorite songs.

We returned to Shanghai when I was just an infant, where I grew (not very tall) and waxed (not very strong) and became very adept in the handling of chopsticks and the singing of "Waltzing Matilda" with a Chinese accent. Pearl Harbor and the resulting Japanese invasion of China caught us in Shanghai. My mother and I were interned as civilian POWs for two and a half years in Yangchow (up the Grand Canal). My father, who served as a lieutenant with the Royal Navy, fought his

11

way through the battle of Hong Kong and was captured and imprisoned there.

All in all our imprisonment turned out to be a very thirsty experience. We were constantly in short supply not only of food, which was bad enough, but even more vital, of WATER also. Water, or lack of it, later affected the total direction of my life. It twisted my psyche and turned my heart into a divining rod which jiggled and went twitch, twitch when I met John Angus—civil engineer, professional *water* conservationist—whose patron saint was Noah, of flood control fame! Our marriage may lack life, liberty, money and the pursuit of happiness. But of one thing I am assured, it shall never lack water. And when it comes down to the nitty gritty, that's what counts! Try not bathing for two and a half years, and you'll see what I mean!

In the foreground, we live in a canyon in California where things that go bump in the night are generally raccoons running across the roof, or coyotes tipping over the hen coop or, on occasion, our son falling out of bed. I have spent the past 15 years being educated into the intriguing, bizarre cultures that flourish in our California canyons, beginning as they did with the flower children a decade ago.

A poster of my life should read "Bloom Where You Are Transplanted," a slogan I firmly believe in! In digging our roots into canyon soil we bloomed two children, Ann (affectionately called "Twinkie") and Ian, both of whom we generally refer to as "those bloomin' kids," (such as in "Where are those bloomin' kids?" or "What have those bloomin' kids done now?").

All this means that we are several thousand poorer in money, but several thousand richer in memories—many of which frolic through the pages of this book.

Up to Heaven and Down to Earth is written as a

companion to my first book *Between Your Status and Your Quo*. I trust they will be good companions and live compatibly, not only on the shelf, but in the hearts of my readers! This book is offered as a primer for practical Christianity and is designed to help us over the hurdles of our day-to-day experiences and on to productive living.

Being a well-rounded author (getting rounder every year), I've written a well-rounded book with a wide range of chapters for everyone from teenagers to theologians. It's a down-to-earth look at our faith, yet reaches up to heaven with an evangelistic wallop!

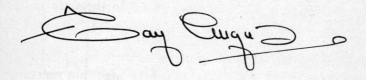

The Light Hand
of God

Research reveals that humor is one of the highest levels of intelligence. Being an aspiring humorist I state that fact with a great deal of gusto! God-consciousness and humor are two of the vital elements that set man apart from the chimpanzee. Animals may laugh, grin, have fun, frolic and enjoy themselves, as evidenced by beavers sliding down a snow bank, but they don't play practical jokes on each other or tell funny stories about the Irishman, Englishman and Scotsman. They don't tell dirty stories either, which is a plus for their side!

All this profundity gives rise to such words as *witless* (without *wit*) and *witty* (with *wit*), also nit*wit* which is sort of a cross between the two. Having a sense of humor boils down to being able to say "tee-hee" instead of "boo-hoo." As a psychological safety valve it is one of the best preventatives for a nervous breakdown.

A recent report out of Australia tells us that doctors on prolonged emergency-room duty have a high suicide rate. This is not funny, it's tragic! I've long wondered how doctors can cope with endless human suffering and still hang in there. A local surgeon I know has pulled emergency-room duty non-stop for some three years now. With a highly developed sense of nonsense, he calls himself an old "sew and sew" and is one of the most fun-loving men you could hope to meet. He often breaks the tension of a situation with a well-timed quip. He is a man of great faith, great compassion, great sensitivity and great *wit*. Eliminate any two of those and he'd probably go bananas.

Queen Victoria ushered in 50 glorious years with the quip, "We are not amused" and kept Englishmen in high-button boots, starched collars and uncomfortable love seats for two-and-a-half prim and proper generations.

Marie Antoinette said "Let them eat cake," a comment which cost her her head and appetite to boot.

The wit of Will Rogers, Winston Churchill and Harry Truman is still making waves in political circles. Churchill once looked at a fellow member of parliament and said, "There but for the grace of God goes God!" A truism still applicable not only to fellow members of various parliaments, but to fellow members of various faiths as well.

God has a terrific sense of humor, the belly-button being proof in point. One only has to sit in the bathtub contemplating his navel for any length of time to be convinced. Now, as if to vindicate the worth of the long-neglected navel, Drs. Herbert and Irving Dardik, cardiovascular surgeons at Montefiore Hospital in New York, are experimenting with veins taken from umbilical cords. Used as substitute leg arteries in cases where arteriosclerosis has resulted in painful ulcers or gangrene, these veins eliminate the need for amputation.

If these transplants continue to prove successful, a prenatal babies' union needs to be formed to ensure a minimum $10 a yard deposit on umbilical cord veins. Such depositions would launch each baby into the world, if not with a silver spoon in its mouth, at least with money in the bank, a good beginning towards a college education. And who knows, after generations of kids putting their good ol' dad out of running condition, they may now be the very means of putting their good ol' dad's legs back into running condition—a welcome change.

The spiritual impact of all this is found in Proverbs 17:22, "A merry heart doeth good like a medicine," and Proverbs 15:13, "A merry heart maketh a cheerful countenance." In contemporary lingo, it's called keeping the *fun* in *fun*damental Christianity.

I don't know what kind of countenances surrounded Solomon, but it's been my observation that cheery countenances, bless them, are ofttimes hiding broken hearts and grim countenances don't always reflect the merry hearts under them. Think of the English bulldog who must be one of the ugliest creatures created. Yet this dear little beastie is a gentle, warm, affectionate pet.

Publishers go to great lengths to match a cover to a book—because people judge a book by its cover. However, when it comes to people, don't.

My husband has the greatest sense of humor and is one of the most fun-loving persons I've ever met. Yet his countenance can only be described as dour Scotch! Handsome, but dour Scotch! Beware of the "dour" Scots—they don't grow thistles, wear kilts and play bagpipes for nothing.

When John and I were first married I used to worry that he was worried. "Is everything all right?" was my constant question.

He finally burst under the pressure: "Good grief, woman, of course everything is all right. Just because I don't go around grinning like a blithering idiot all the time doesn't mean that I'm not happy!"

His response was reassuring, and now that I've grown accustomed to his face I'm not misled by a few misplaced wrinkles, frowns and periodic twitches. As a matter of fact, I'm so confident in his contentment that he has to throw a fit of mock apoplexy when he wants to let me know something is indeed wrong!

The "good medicine" of a merry heart is the tonic that took many of us through the traumas of a Japanese concentration camp in World War II. Fellowship is forged on the joys as well as the sorrows of living. A circulated joke, cartoon or *bon mot* often broke the oppression of our ordeal and lifted our hopes anew.

The first weeks of weevils in our gruel revolted our palates. However, when hunger took over we not only chuckled at the weevils, we also laughed off the little worms that frequently showed up in our food and swallowed them down heartily as an extra source of protein.

After a terrible drought, when we were rationed to two cups of water per day for everything (you brushed your teeth and swallowed!), a young woman in the camp went momentarily berserk and jumped into the tank containing our dwindling water supply—clothes and all. We said, "Ah well, these things happen" and drank it anyway. No one was angry with her, we understood, forgave and chuckled.

I grew up with the "glad" game of Pollyanna. But our children have Mary Poppins, her "spoonful of sugar" and "I Love to Laugh." Either way we try and let a bit

WHEN HUNGER TOOK OVER, WE LAUGHED AT THE WEEVILS
AND JUST SAW THEM AS "EXTRA PROTEIN."

of mirth deflect some of our defects. Our children milk this to the full: "A funny thing just happened—I accidentally ripped the screen on my bedroom window!"

"Another funny thing is about to happen," retort I, "bend over!"

So on and so forth. . . .

♪✳-#-!-"♪♪♪((✳-#-!-"?is the garbled lingo of teenagers—step one in the generation gap—their popular means of communication. I dedicate this chapter to all teenagers, past, present and future, anywhere. Also to adults who like to behave like teenagers.

♪✳-#-!-"♪♪♪((✳-#-!-"?is a universal teen language and, translated, means "a rose by any other name is called a tulip." It also means "sticks and stones can break my bones, but words hurt me most of all."

I find teens a curious species and enjoy talking to them, with them and—within our own family circle—at them. Teens are God's test of your faith. It's not that He has to know how much you can endure, He already knows that. Rather it's that He wants *you* to know how much you can endure and, now that the Spanish Inquisition is over, He uses teens to help you discover your endurance-ability.

A few parents have sent their teens to me for counseling, which makes it difficult, because then I don't know where to send my own teens for counseling. So instead of counseling mine, I threaten to squeeze their blackheads just before a date and to buy them lots of books by Dr. S. Haim Ginott and Clyde Narramore.

But I love counseling teens. The first thing we do is sign a mutual affidavit of amnesia to forget everything we say to each other. Then we sit and smirk for a while —they smirk while I talk, and I smirk while they talk. We usually come away very good friends, also very good smirkers.

We talk about boys (girls), sex, alcohol, drugs, smoking, marijuana, Alice Cooper and parents, in that order. If you're a parent you may note the order of priority. The astounding fact is that Christian teens talk about exactly the same things as non-Christian teens—they may not do exactly the same things, but they talk about them.

The most important question I ever ask teenagers is, "What is the most valuable thing you own?"

No matter how they answer me, I tell them that, without a shadow of a doubt, the most valuable thing *I* own, have owned or shall ever own is my *reputation*. It bears repeating—*the most valuable thing a man has is his reputation*. Shakespeare in *Othello* says, "Who steals my purse steals trash; . . . But he who filches from me my good name robs me of that which not enriches him and makes me poor indeed."

We have a reputation before God, our Creator; we have a reputation before Jesus Christ, our Saviour, if we are Christians. Indeed we carry the reputation of His name upon us before the world. We have a reputation before ourselves to the highest or lowest of our ability and we live within the standard we have set. We have a reputation before our parents and reflect their reputation. And we have a reputation before our friends, strangers, community and world at large. I caution teenagers to weigh the action of their lives in this knowledge, and then I tell them, "Don't blow it!"

Fortunately, a reputation is something that is built, day by day and year by year. If it has been ruined in the past it can be reconstructed to even greater glory in the future. Unfortunately, its circulation is dependent upon many people and this is where the interplay of what Paul calls "idle words" of Christian conversation is a most grievous sin. The world calls it gossip. James 3:8 calls the tongue "an unruly evil full of deadly poison." The Christian who has bridled his tongue has tamed his whole body (see Jas. 3:2).

I have heard the whispers, seen the arched eyebrows, the peculiar smiles, the twitching mouth and blinking eyes of teens talking about other teens. I have also heard the whispers, seen the arched eyebrows, the peculiar smiles, the twitching mouth and blinking eyes of adults talking about other adults. I have seen vulnerable reputations floating along waves of jealousies, irritations, anger and just plain meanness.

My guardian angel cringes whenever I open my mouth and, I think, would gladly give me a mild case of lockjaw much of the time. May God forgive me.

While speaking to a group of youngsters during Vacation Bible School one summer I had our college-age students hide in the balcony of the church and, on a given cue, blow thousands of bubbles down to the sanctuary below. As they floated down I told the kids, "These are the words you speak. Now try and catch them all and put them back in the bottles!"

I caution teenagers to *please be careful whom you confide in!* Probably the best confidant a teen can have is a pen pal 10,000 miles away. Parents *should be* a kid's best confidant. But unfortunately, this is not always the case, for some parents are totally indiscriminate with their child's sacred confidence.

Occasionally we call this laxity "prayer requests." Now, the prayers of devout brethren move the hand of God and are our most coveted gifts to one another; but be careful into whose hands you place your most sacred trust. While the spirit is indeed willing, the flesh is weak, and your confidence to a weak brother may result in shattering, devastating consequences. Be careful that you don't betray your child and at the same time cause someone to sin against you by burdening him with a confidence he is unable to handle.

Another thing I have become aware of in teen counseling is that *parents lay maturities upon their children beyond their years.* How my heart has been blessed over and over again as I have joined in a prayer of forgiveness spoken from the pulpit by Rev. Bob Schaper: "God forgive us for expecting our children to be adults." Parents are guilty of this too frequently.

We are foremost ambassadors of ourselves. Build a good reputation and we make a good representation:

"Sow a thought and reap an act;
Sow an act and reap a habit;
Sow a habit and reap a character;
Sow a character and reap a destiny."

A Chinese sage of the sixteenth century B.C. said, "I meet good with good that good may be maintained; I meet evil with good that good may be created." There is never any excuse for bad conduct. It's a deliberate choice and invariably the person to whom it's most devastating is oneself.

When I was 18 years old I wrote down a prayer by Henry Wright of Yale and it became a goal in my life—and still is:

"I will live my life for God, for others rather than for myself, for the advancement of the Kingdom of God rather than for my personal success. I will not drift into my life work, but I will do my utmost by prayer, investigation, meditation and service to discover that form and place of life work in which I can become of the largest use to the Kingdom of God. As I find it I will follow it under the leadership of Jesus, wheresoever it takes me, cost what it may."[1]

Footnote

1. Charles T. Holman, *Psychology and Religion for Everyday Living* (New York: Macmillan and Company, 1949), p. 145.

Proverbs $2 a Dozen

Scripture buffs have designed 101 different ways to memorize Bible verses. I have taken my daily "vitamin" and have spent summers with cards propped up on the window sill above my kitchen sink determined to stencil favorite passages of Scripture indelibly on my brain. They have long been "hid in my heart" (Ps. 119:11); the trouble is remembering just where I hid them when I want to find them. Conversion of the desires of my heart to the disciplines of my mind is the problem. John 3:16 and Romans 8:28 are easy—they're short and snappy. But how I stand in awe of brethren who recite not just Romans 8:28 but the whole of Romans 8!

It's not only *memorizing* the Scripture, it's *finding* Habakkuk 3:11 or Amos 9:15. (Actually it's finding

Habakkuk or Amos at all that worries me.) Fortunately or unfortunately, I'm not alone. A member of our choir —sitting up there and facing all of us in the congregation —sometimes has trouble finding the Scripture the Pastor said to turn to. So he just pretends he's found it immediately and lets his eyes follow along imaginary lines in Ezekiel, when he's really turned to Proverbs. Then, when he has a chance he slowly sneaks his pages back and forth until he hits the right passage.

Little does he know I bluff too—with his hymns. When I can't reach that high "C" I just open my mouth wide and give the impression of great effortless range while not a note comes out. And he stands up there thinking, "Why hasn't Fay joined the choir? She sings with such ease."

This summer I decided to concentrate on complete victory in memorizing Scripture. "Satan does not want us memorizing God's Word," I told the family. "He fogs our minds and muddles our memory. Well, are we going to let that devil get the better of us?"

"No, we will not admit defeat," I continued. "We will fight in the living room, we will fight in the dining room, we will fight in the morning, we will fight in the evening. I offer you blood, toil, tears and sweat."

The kids were rolling their eyes at each other and tapping their fingers on the table, totally unappreciative of original oratory!

"Not only will we win the victory, but I will offer $2 *a dozen for memorized proverbs!*"

Eyeballs snapped back into their sockets and finger tapping stopped.

"How much?"

"$2 a dozen, cold, hard cash."

"Is 'the wages of sin is death' worth a dime?" asked Ian.

"No sir," I smirked, "I'm only forking out for proverbs this month."

I thought of all the juicy ones I'd zap into their psyche: "A soft answer turneth away wrath: but grievous words stir up anger" (Prov. 15:1). That should settle all the grievous words that stir up anger around the bathroom early in the morning.

"Hear, ye children, the instruction of a father" (Prov. 4:1).

"He that spareth his rod hateth his son: but he that loveth him chasteneth him betimes" (Prov. 13:24). It would be worth $2 alone to hear Ian recite that one!

"Her children arise up, and call her blessed; her husband also, and he praiseth her" (Prov. 31:28).

"Favor is deceitful, and beauty is vain: but a woman that feareth the Lord, she shall be praised" (Prov. 31:30). Beauty and favor! Hah, let them try to tell me I'm getting fat and sassy after that!

Within a week Ian shrugged up. The "shrug" is the latest 11-year-old strut—he jiggled his shoulders and shuffled his feet. "How much will you pay for three proverbs?"

"Nothing," I snapped back, "nothing flat. It's a dozen or zero—Z-E-R-O!"

A wicked gleam came into his eyes. "Well, if you won't pay me for three proverbs, how much will you pay me to forget I ever read Song of Solomon?" I whacked him hard.

This is our son, the ultimate con artist. Our daughter Twinkie, on the other hand, has always displayed great moral integrity and ethics. She memorized her weekly Scripture verses to the glory of God, shunning any proffered Sunday School talent reward, until Ian persuaded her to take the talents anyway which he would then add to his meager pile. At the end of the season he could be seen visiting the talent redemption center and coming out with pockets full of trinkets as a tribute to his sister's memory.

Scripture songs have been the best additive to church since the invention of disposable communion cups. Through the creativity of the Jesus generation we are singing "Thy lovingkindness is better than life" (Ps. 63:3); "Surely goodness and mercy shall follow me all the days, all the days of my life" (see Ps. 23:6); "Rejoice in the Lord, always; and again I say, Rejoice" (Phil. 4:4); "Now unto the King, eternal, immortal, invisible, the only wise God, be honor and glory for ever and ever. Amen" (1 Tim. 1:17).

One of my favorites is from Galatians 5:1, "Stand fast therefore in the liberty [clap, clap, clap] wherewith Christ hath made us free [clap, clap, clap] and be not entangled again with the yoke of [clap] bondage!"

Of course I've got into the habit of being able to quote Galatians 5:1 only when I clap at all the appropriate times. This bothers a few people, but all in all it's very effective.

The commercial community has long realized the power of a jingle promoting a product, from Pepsi to Campbell's Soup. Get our youth singing the Scriptures and they'll never forget them. Let the Bible be their hymnbook!

Subconscious saturation was a trick tried by a young Christian brother, called Peter, living in a commune in Glendale, California. He was so anxious to fill his mind with the Word of God that he hooked up a tape recorder, read whole books of the Bible into it, and then put on earphones and slept with the tape playing into his subconscious night after night. Peter said he'd have the loveliest dreams—the Lord would be walking with him blessing the lilies of the field or feeding the 5,000.

Then one night he sat bolt upright at about 3:00 A.M. with terrifying rock music pounding full blast into his head, shaking him violently. He shouted out rebuking Satan, claiming deliverance and quoted Scripture at the top of his voice to no avail. Then he opened his eyes and saw the other brothers sharing his room buckled over with laughter. They had jokingly altered his tape to interrupt his night's Scripture with stereo sound. May the Lord forgive them!

The power of the Word of God cannot be over-estimated. I once visited a young man who claimed to belong to Satan and who worshiped Hermes. Just 21 years old, he was handsome and brilliantly clever.

This young man had built himself an ornately carved gypsy-type camper shell over the back of his pickup truck. He traveled the country in this vehicle telling tarot cards for a living. In a single afternoon, he made as much as $40.

With him in the camper was a large ceramic statue of his deity which he had creatively designed and molded himself. He had also designed a chess set with hollow pieces that could be filled with hashish. As a game progressed, the winner of each piece would sniff the hash, and the game would intensify.

I had stumbled on this devotee of the devil while looking for someone else. So I asked our assistant pastor Stan to come visit him with me. In his camper, we told the young man we were Christians and asked if he had a Bible.

He fairly vomited at our mention of the Bible. "I travel under the manifesto of Satan," he said. "Hermes is my god. I wouldn't have a Bible in here."

Now I have the blood of the Battle of Trafalgar in my veins, and when someone says they travel under the manifesto of Satan and wouldn't look at a Bible, them thar's fightin' words. Satan is a liar and a cheat. And it was obvious that this young man was in bondage to the devil's lies and delusions.

"Are you familiar with the Greek philosophers?" we asked.

"Yes, I am."

"You remind me somewhat of the philosophers on Mars' Hill," I said. We opened our New Testament and read aloud from Acts 17 the discourse of Paul on Mars' Hill.

"Is that in the Bible?" he asked.

"Yes," we responded, and without further comment we excused ourselves. Our time had been stretched and we could not stay longer. But we had planted a seed that would need watering.

We had to get this young man a Bible, Stan and I agreed. And no ordinary Bible would do. He'd probably pitch a paperback edition of *Good News for Modern Man* into the trash. And he'd undoubtedly do likewise with a black, zippered *King James*. No, the Word of God needed to pierce this heart in an unusual way. He was a most unusual man and responded to unusual approaches.

I prayed about it for a day and then made the decision. I would buy this man the most beautiful edition of the Bible I could find. I rushed over to the Nazarene bookstore and there it was—a large, gorgeous, richly bound, red-letter edition, illustrated with reproductions of great masterpieces and the words *Holy Bible* in gold on the cover. Only $32.

Thirty-two dollars! How on earth could I explain spending $32 out of my household budget on a Bible for a stranger, and a deluded stranger at that?

But the Lord spoke to my heart and said, "Fay, I don't expect you to use your money for this. Make me a loan and I will return it to you." Now God always pays His debts and His credit is the best we can have.

I talked it over with Stan and he agreed, "I believe you're right, Fay," he said, "I'll back you up in whatever way I can."

We approached Pastor and asked if we could tell the story at prayer meeting that night and then leave a plate at the door for anyone who would like to be part of God's loan.

"Let me get this straight," he said. "You're buying a $32 Bible for a man who you say is traveling under the 'manifesto of Satan,' who worships the god Hermes and who might even have left town by the time you take it to him?"

"That's right," I said.

He shook his head slowly, "I'll have to pray about this. I'll let you know tonight."

I used our grocery money to buy the Bible. We inscribed the presentation page and took it out to the camper. Jim was there, getting ready to pull out to Big Sur that night.

"We've brought you a present," we said, as we went in and handed him the huge unwrapped book with its *Holy Bible* blazing gold before him.

He took it in his hands, the hands that had molded Hermes, the hands that had hollowed chess pieces for hashish, the hands that dealt tarot cards. He took the HOLY BIBLE into those hands, opened it and was speechless.

After a moment he stammered, "You mean this is for *me?*"

"Yes," we replied. "We hope you'll read it."

"But, but—it's so beautiful. It must be very expensive." A look of bewildered wonder came over his face.

"The words of Jesus are all printed in red," we said.

"You can just turn to the back portion of the book and read in red what Jesus says."

"Is the part you read to me the other day here?" he said.

"Yes," we said and found and marked it for him—*Paul on Mars' Hill.*

"Wow," he said. "Wow, I'll treasure this, I'll even sleep on it—maybe *it'll blow some of the evil out of my mind!*"

"Sleep on it if you like, Jim, but read it."

"For sure," he said. "For sure that'll blow some of the evil out of my mind."

That night at prayer meeting I entered late and sat at the back. They were singing the closing stanza of a hymn, and I'm sure Pastor Bob felt my gaze burning through the back of his neck as he sat in the front row. He turned his head, saw me, grinned and nodding his affirmation mouthed the word yes. Praise the Lord!

I shared the story with the brethren present, we left a plate out and the Lord provided $36—the cost, the tax and interest on my loan to Him. A young man who swore he would never have a Bible defile his habitation now had holy writ in his hands. He had promised to read it. He was going to use it to pillow his confused head, and he had cried out to God the Father, "Maybe it'll blow some of the evil out of my mind."

We pray it has.

Proverbs, $2 a dozen, anyone?

The Wages of Sin
Are Very Expensive

My husband and I recently calculated that over the past 10 years we have saved $3,000 just by not smoking. The average American family spends $25 a month on liquor. That comes to $300 a year, or another $3,000 over a 10-year period, and this is based on a minimal non-addictive consumption. By the time we've been married 20 years we will have saved $12,000 just by avoiding these two vices alone! If we are blessed with 40 years together, it will amount to a saving of $24,000!

When a young person asks me about smoking and drinking the first thing I say is "They're addictive and very expensive!" Then I elaborate on the above figures and ask, "If you had $12,000 in hand in 10 years, what would you like to do with it?"

Boy, do I get creative answers—a speedboat, a trip to

Zanzibar, a fantastic car.... It's motivational—money, that is! If you regularly bank your urges you'll be making a wise investment that will pay off handsomely over the years.

The most over-budgeted and under-emphasized sin in the average American household is that of gluttony. Having just finished a steak dinner complete with french fries and strawberry shortcake dessert, I can state that fact with a great deal of authority! And gluttony *is* a sin, have no doubt about it. Proverbs 23:21 says, "For the drunkard and the glutton shall come to poverty." And in Philippians 3:19, Paul speaks of those whose "God is their belly."

I have sat through banquet after banquet and have cringed every time the host or hostess prays, "And bless this food to our body's use...."

I hurriedly whisper "Please don't, dear God. What most of our bodies really can't use right now is all this food!"

In our home we've taken to just thanking God for the abundance of food He has provided on our overladen table and ask His help in disciplining us not to eat too much of it! I wonder what would happen if we all ate only when we were hungry—we'd probably get by with just one good lip-smackin' meal a day; instead, we're all munching and crunching our way to obesity!

Gluttony isn't just limited to the fat man, either. I've seen many gluttonous thin men, it's just that their metabolism is different and it doesn't show as much!

The World Vision telethons on hunger are impact programs that should lead to a nationwide fast! During one telethon our 10-year-old son was so moved by the starvation of the hunger belt that he phoned in to commit $1 a month to help "feed the hungry people of the world." This was no small offering as he's not on an allowance and has to earn whatever money he has. The slogan around our home is "Them that don't work, don't eat" (See 2 Thess. 3:10). His most regular source of income is earned by washing the family car once a week —he pledged one car wash a month to the hungry.

In a recent letter to Mr. Mooneyham of World Vision, Ian said: "And please keep on feeding the hungry people of the world. I don't like being hungry. As a matter of fact right now *I could use a little hunger* as I'm getting too fat!"

Most all of us could "use a little hunger" now and then. Gluttony? Starve it to death!

As I see the $s and ¢s whizzing across our divorce courts with settlements out of court and settlements in court, alimonies, child supports, division of properties, establishments of new bachelor quarters, there is one unavoidable answer: *it's cheaper to reconcile!* I groan at the enormous waste of it all. That's the Scot in me! Strangely enough, were the same financial frivolity invested in one's present mate and family, rather than trying to get rid of them, happiness nine times out of ten would sneak up from the rear and say "Boo! You haven't lost me after all!"

Tripping the light fantastic with a gal under your arm costs money—plenty! And the resulting legal involvement costs plenty more on a continuous basis. "All right," you snap back, "money can't buy happiness!"

"True," I retort, "but, to quote a purloined quip, 'the only trouble with happiness is it can't buy money!' "

You pays your money and you takes your choice! Love on a shoestring doesn't have such a good track record either, especially with a couple of broken hearts at either end. Financial problems are one of the major reasons why so many marriages self-destruct.

Invest in your spouse, your family and yourself—it

pays off in both money and relationships. If we put the same effort into impressing our loved ones as we do total strangers, who don't give a whit about us and can't even remember our names six months hence, we will have a hundredfold increase in personal happiness. When I am tempted to knock my family and relatives I ask myself, "Who is going to bury me?" They are, and no one else—under normal circumstances, of course. Your husband, your wife, your children and your close kith and kin—please be nice to them!

I have observed second courtships over the past few years—in singles groups where guys and gals try to make the best impression possible on each other. And they're so nice to each other's kids, it's beautiful. But I can't help wonder if these same courtesies and niceties had been given to their original spouses and their own children, what would have happened in their first marriages?

My husband walked in one night, irritated by a long stint in the office, and proceeded to chew out our son in a way that made my motherhood instincts bristle. When we got into bed later, I commented, "You know, if you were courting me and I heard you speak to my children that way, no way would I consider marrying you!"

It jolted him. And it jolted me as I reversed the situation and remembered the many times when the shoe was on the other foot, and he had to witness my railings around the home. Were we courting, the impression would have been very negative. Well, we still are courting, and the niceties still apply, only more so now.

Speak to your office help the way you sometimes speak to your wife, and they'd turn on their heels·and walk out! We wouldn't dream of doing it, would we? No, because we maintain good manners in public. But since

41

when is being married any excuse for bad manners in private?

Courtesy costs nothing and buys a whole lot. So treat your wife the way you'd treat a girl friend, and your wife will become your girl friend. Treat your husband the way you would treat a lover, and your husband will become your lover—if he isn't already. You say, "I can't afford it."

I say, "Be careful, or you may have to afford it with someone else!"

This doesn't mean that you can't relax and be yourself in your own home. Heaven forbid! It just means that you must change your present self into a nicer self. Then the relaxing will take care of itself and be far more enjoyable!

One of the good things about the near-extinct civilization of British colonialism is that it did teach one how to behave graciously—rawther too much at times, but rawther nice all the same. I even find myself saying "Excuse me" to the dog when he's lying in my way. Silly, but it's better than kicking him. And his disposition is the better for it. He's a charming dog.

Things of "Good Report"

We are living in a valley of the shadow of death.

Headlines blaze the bad news of the world, murders, atrocities, perversions, corruptions, violence. Their effects infiltrate our circle of friends and our families. They infiltrate our fellowship of the church, as life touches life and our arms lift up with the prayer from our depth, "Have mercy on us, O God, our Father."

I have stood with the tears streaming down my face and shared with brethren the agony of the knowledge of Satan worship in our local cemetery. I have winced at the jewelry of human knucklebones worn as necklaces and bracelets. I have known about the rape of a baby.

The crushing circumstances of degenerate man have stretched my spirit until my soul bled. I have cried for days and tossed in sleepless nights.

Growing up in the cultural deformities of disease-riddled and poverty-stricken China and suffering through man's inhumanity to man during the war years was small preparation indeed for the subcultures of our American society. Here, in our good earth, my heart has broken. I have never been ashamed of my tears, rather I have been ashamed that more have not wept. Where is the "goodness and mercy" that should "follow me, all the days of my life"?

The yang and the yin of all things bright and beautiful against all things putrid and horrible fractured my faith until St. Paul pulled me out: "Finally, brethren, whatsoever things are true, whatsoever things are honest, whatsoever things are just, whatsoever things are pure, whatsoever things are lovely, whatsoever things are of *good report;* if there be any virtue and if there be any praise, *think on these things*" (Phil. 4:8, italics added). This is the Bible verse that has most often mended my heart. Whatsoever things are of "good report . . . think on these things." A lifeline to sanity!

Even as Jesus wept over Jerusalem (Luke 19:41), we must weep over the problems of our day. But do not dwell on the macabre. Yes, our spirits *may* be broken and our hearts *must* ache through all the suffering of the world. For we dare not forget—I pray I never forget—the suffering of the world. Jesus doesn't.

And we alleviate where we can. But then we must lay it all at the feet of our Lord and Saviour and pass—not on, but through. There is a difference. To pass on is to observe and not be touched; to pass through is to experience.

Complacency has no part in Christianity, but man is

not strong enough to bear the brunt of sin. Strange how we can endure our own personal griefs and pains; it is the griefs and pains of those we love that break us. I recall the man who was tied to a tree in Hong Kong during the war. His wife, a nurse, was tied to another tree and he was forced to watch while 50 soldiers raped her. He went insane. The psychology of sadism is very effective.

I confess I could not endure. I listen in frightened awe to braggart saints who swear that nothing, nowhere could ever make them renounce Christ. Peter said the same thing once (see Matt. 26:33–35). My heart shall never renounce Christ, but my lips could be persuaded to. If they take your child and say, "Renounce or we'll cut off a hand," you may hold firm. And they will cut off the hand. Then they say, "Renounce, or we'll cut off the other hand," you may still hold firm. But there will be a point of mutilation at which you will break.

I would break at the first hand and I believe Jesus would understand, forgive my lips and read only my suffering heart. I even believe that is what He would want me to do. My own hands I could freely forfeit. But those of my child—perhaps his eyes, or ears or feet as well? Fortunately, at a given stress our sanity snaps.

"Come unto me, all ye that labour and are heavy laden, and I will give you rest" (Matt. 11:28). Twice recently I have heard of murders of young Christian women. "I can't handle it," a distraught relative of one cried to me. "It's too much. I can't take this!"

Of course she couldn't. Neither could I. We took the heavy burden and laid it on our Lord. We passed through the heartbreak in prayer. And we put our thoughts on "whatsoever things are of good report."

Psychologists tell us to relive the pleasant experiences of our life, over and over. A therapeutic massage of our memory. I recall a friend telling me of her childhood at the seashore in England. One morning while just a small girl, she lay quietly in an empty rowboat moored by the beach and listened to the lap of the gentle water rock its hull. "Even now when I shut my eyes and think back," says Vonnie, "I can still feel the motion of the boat and hear the soothing lap of the waves. I can even smell the tarp that pillowed my head. It was one of the quietest and loveliest moments of my life!"

A few years ago my daughter won a lovely trophy—it was totally unexpected and the happiness of the surprise continues to be relived by us over and over again.

"Remember how you felt when they called your name?"

"What did you think when you went forward?"

"What were you thinking, mom?"

"I was so proud of you!" And on and on, reliving the joy.

After 17 years of marriage my husband and I still recall the moment we fell in love and the times of our courtship, and the birth of our babies. Sometimes at night I relive the happy moments in the delivery room when the doctor placed that new little life on my abdomen and said, "It's a girl, Mrs. Angus." Or in Ian's case, when I noticed first and said "Hallelujah, doctor, it's a boy!"

Remembering the "good report" of pleasant interpersonal relationships modifies our anger and irritations. A woman came to me with bitter complaints against her teenage daughter. After listening for a short time I asked her, "What is the happiest moment you and your daughter have ever shared?" She thought a second and then recalled a special occasion.

"OK, now tell me the nicest thing she has ever done for you." Again another moment relived.

"Can you remember when she was born? Tell me about it."

"What was she like as a toddler?" We dipped into reservoirs of love for half an hour and by the time the lady got back to the crises of her daughter's current misbehavior, her attitudes and feelings towards her had changed from resentment to compassion and understanding.

How often do you relive the memory and "good report" of your salvation and commitment to Jesus Christ? In his *Jesus Person Maturity Manual*, David Wilkerson takes us through those moments:

> Your prayer for salvation spanned the universe, touched the heart of God and set off a chain reaction throughout heaven.
>
> Your sins were wiped away from the book of judgment and your name inscribed in the book of life. God the Father, the Son and the Holy Ghost—yes, the Godhead—came down and made their abode in your heart.
>
> A guardian angel was sent to build a wall of fire round about you. In the Father's house of many mansions a place for you was being readied. Angel choirs began to rejoice and sing hallelujahs to the King of Glory, over the lost sheep that was found.
>
> Your tears were bottled and saved. Your words of sorrow and repentance were recorded as eternal tones that will never die. Christ, the intercessor, began to pray for you and to present your name before the Father, for He once said, "I pray for them which Thou hast given to me—that Thou shouldst keep them from the wicked one." It is true—God is eter-

nally bound by His Word to respond to the sinner's prayer.

Your prayer moved all of heaven and created a great stir.[1]

I read this regularly, probably once every two or three months. I recall the moment of my salvation—the best of all the "good reports" in my life—and with welled-up eyes I go to my knees and once again I thank Him.

Footnote

1. David Wilkerson, *Jesus Person Maturity Manual* (Glendale: Regal Books Division, G/L Publications, 1971) p. 1.

Eenie, Meenie, Miney and Who?

The most glaring omission in the current push on women's liberation is their failure to eliminate the word "men" from women. As any self-respecting feminist will agree, there is something about the word "men" that curdles her curls. But erase "men" from women and you reduce us to wo.

And what can you do with a wo? Add the wrong suffix, for instance, and your wo comes out woozy. Reverse your wo, and you have ow! More than one man is going around saying. "Ow, ow, ow," because he reversed his wo!

So men, just be very careful how you handle your wos. Handle us right, and we come out as wonderful and wow!

The favorite word in wo circles is the word word. A

MEN, BE VERY CAREFUL HOW YOU HANDLE YOUR WO'S.

wo and her *wo*rds are never—repeat—never parted. She is as much an origin of them as they are an extension of her.

Only a *wo* is capable of a one-party dialogue with her husband. The dialogue usually begins, "I'd like to have a few *wo*rds with you—!" and is punctuated with such phrases as, "And by the way—" or "And one more thing—!" It generally ends with one or the other sleeping on the living room couch for two nights.

Amen would naturally become A*wo* in an equal opportunity church, and when pronounced in unison by all the *wo*s in the congregation could give God the impression that there is a bad case of the sneezes going around!

With volleys of discrimination and equality being shot from both sides in the war of the sexes, and with our vocabulary now sporting such modifications as "chairperson," "newsperson," etc., the differentiating nouns "male-female, man-woman" may in time be totally erased from our dictionary. How on earth the earth of the future will be propagated without alternative genders is a conundrum.

Of course, if the volleys of discrimination and equality are shot too far and, if the gay liberation movement is predominant in our society at that time, babies will already have become an endangered species by then. Gay libbers invented zero-population growth. Perhaps we should infiltrate their demonstrations with picket signs saying "Unfair to the Unborn."

The crux of the whole matter is that we are already teetering on the brink of a unisex society. And now with every Eenie, Meenie, Miney and Whoever pressure group lobbying their position and screaming their credibility, *Homo sapiens* are rapidly degenerating into homo-saps!

"Discrimination" is one of the largest words being

thrown around today. Unfortunately, it is being associated with a lot of negatives when actually it is representative of very honorable virtues. Synonyms of *to discriminate* are "to differentiate," "to distinguish" and "to discern." So a discriminating person is one who carefully weighs choices.

I teach my children to weigh choices. I teach them to discriminate between good and evil. I teach them to be discriminating in their choice of life-style, their choice of literature, their choice of entertainment, their choice of friends, etc. I hope to lead them into maturity by showing them how to weigh the differences of any given circumstances.

Discrimination is an essential if we are to protect the moral fibre of our society against blights such as perversion, pornography and prostitution. The September 8, 1975 issue of *Time* magazine stated the shocking fact that 100,000 American *boys* between the ages of 13 and 16 were actively engaged in prostitution—an instant replay of ancient Rome. The United States is in the middle of the worst epidemic of VD that it has ever known. Yet smut peddlers are springing up on every corner and "Adult" Theaters have been assigned special advertising sections in our local newspapers in which to promote their erotic, hard-core films.

To lack discrimination and take the lid off morality will lead us back to the decadence that felled the Roman Empire. The gay society is nothing new. Its roots were bred in Sodom, and its blight infiltrated Athenian temples and Roman Senates. Men and women driven by deviate lusts bred the debauchery that weakened and collapsed the strongest nations that ever ruled.

Corinth was a hotbed of perversion. So was Rome. Paul writes to the Romans: "For even their women did change the natural use into that which is against nature:

And likewise also the men, leaving the natural use of the woman, burned in their lust one toward another; men with men working that which is unseemly, and receiving in themselves that recompense of their error which was meet" (Rom. 1:26,27).

Perversion is a legacy we need to disinherit. It is disturbing to see Christian theologies and morals modified to convenience the homosexual believer. Recently the Gay Liberation Front demonstrated against the Church, blaming St. Paul of prejudicing Christians against them through his writings. But Paul is not their only accuser. The record of human history alone nullifies their collective worth to any society—religious or secular.

Statistics verify that the majority of homosexuals in our society were not born with their abnormalities—as they often claim. Rather, they were lured, led, educated or forced into a pattern of performance that resulted in a bondage from which they, of their own strength, were not able to free themselves.

Yet an individual caught in the web of the gay society may and can be disentangled. There is a hope, there is a solution, there is a cure through the transforming power of the Holy Spirit of God. And the only criterion for the cure is the desire for deliverance. There is a choice. But it must be the right choice.

Perversion is a choice, and it is the wrong choice. Pornography is a choice, and it is the wrong choice. Prostitution is a choice, and it is the wrong choice.

Total and complete renewal is also a choice. And it is the right choice. And it is also possible. "If any man be in Christ, he is a *new creature: old things* [including perversions] are passed away; behold, all things are become new" (2 Cor. 5:17, italics added).

"Equality!" is another loud shout coming from fist-shaking Eenie, Meenie, Miney and Whoevers around the world. "*Liberté, fraternité, égalité!*" was the slogan of the French Revolution, and we continue to scream it in all languages, colors and creeds. But look who wants equality. Even Satan worshipers are demanding equal rights to worship whomever and however they please. So on and so forth.

Unfortunately, not all persons have been created equal. I have been trying to persuade my husband for years that I am completely equal to Raquel Welch, but with no success whatever. As a matter of fact, he says that the more years pass the more unequal I become with all my lumps and bumps in the wrong places.

In my dancing days, I tried to persuade the Royal Ballet that I was completely equal to Margot Fonteyn. Not so, they said. She had talent.

On the employment front we have the workers and the shirkers. The shirkers are totally unequal to the workers in terms of dollars-and-cents-per-capita output. And yet our personnel rolls are padded with shirkers of all races, colors and creeds, who are dug in deep and waving the whip of *equality* over the heads of their employers!

The United States is a nation of immigrants from all over the world and our basic American skills and characteristics have evolved from this conglomerate. This is good and is part of our strength. However, we are now in danger of fragmenting ourselves into a nation of separate so-called minorities stomping out rights from a wide range of national, ethnic, sexual and social platforms, each group seeking to equalize and promote their cause. And everybody's in the act from Grey Panthers to ERAers.

Indeed, when all the national and social minorities have been sifted to the periphery, just who in fact comprise the *majority* of our population? Christians are certainly considered a national minority in the spiritual spectrum. Jesus knew this and He joined us all in the most perfect equality the world has ever known when He prayed, "That they all may be one; as thou, Father, art in me, and I in thee, that they also may be one in us" (John 17:21).

The only credible equality of achievement may be summed up in the word *merit*. We must merit the right to be selected and acclaimed on all levels of performance. England's Margaret Thatcher has risen from the conservative ranks as a member of parliament and now stands on the threshold of being the first woman prime minister in the history of Great Britain. She has earned recognition through merit, not because she is a woman. The merit of 16 years in the House of Commons, passing her bar examinations as a lawyer, and the excellence of prepared debate and performance on the House floor won her the respect of her party.

Dr. Ralph Bunche won the respect of the world through his years in the United Nations, not because he was black, but because he was better!

When we have overcome the stumbling blocks for a desegregated society and can judge a person's worth by his individual merit rather than having to weigh him on the basis of his gender or ethnic or social background; when we can eliminate the need to balance our personnel scales with per capita number of blacks, whites or albinos and can choose instead the best person for the job, *then* the vigor of our nation's productivity will peak to new heights of achievement.

7

No One's in the Kitchen with Martha!

If someone had been in the kitchen with Martha, toot-in' on his ol' ram's horn, maybe she wouldn't have been so cranky. As it was, she had to go it all alone.

Early that morning, Lazarus had dusted off his best suit and announced, "Guess who's coming to dinner? Lord of lords, King of kings, the Master—that's who."

Now women are programmed to respond to this type of challenge with a chain reaction of activity ranging from enduring two hours in pin curls to polishing all the silver to vacuuming out the fireplace. Inbred within our psyche is the desire to be the hostess with the mostes'.

Martha was no exception. The house had to look its best. She had to look her best. And dinner had to be the best, the very best, with grape leaf dolma and deep fried mackerel to say nothing of hors d'oeuvres of dates and fig newtons.

Three more wrinkles left three permanent creases on her forehead as a result of coordinating the occasion. Her culinary efforts were reaching perfection, but timing was critical. And where was Mary? Sitting in the living room twiddling her thumbs, adoring her Lord—that's where!

Martha said, "Pss-s-t, pss-s-t, pss-s-t," three times from the kitchen door and waved her fork to get Mary's attention, but no luck. That girl was beyond human communication. Finally in desperation she whipped off her apron and went marchin' in. "Wait 'til Jesus hears about this," she thought. "Me sweating over a hot stove all day, and junior miss out there goofing off!"

"Lord, dost thou not care that my sister hath left me to serve alone? bid her therefore that she help me" (Luke 10:40).

The eyes turned full upon her and heaven spoke her name, "Martha, Martha," (twice) "thou art careful and troubled about many things: But one thing is needful: and Mary hath chosen that good part, which shall not be taken away from her" (Luke 10:41,42).

"Well, I never—"

Now, if Jesus had said that to *me* I would have let the mackerel burn, put a notice on the dining room table, "Man shall not live by bread alone," served ice water as the main course and joined the discussion group at the Master's feet. As another hostess once said to her guests, "I suppose you're all wondering how I can spend the cocktail hour with you and still serve a delicious full-course dinner. The truth is, I can't. We're having bananas on cereal!"

Despite the progressive conveniences of the twentieth century, the average housewife continues to be "cumbered about much serving." Not only much serving, but much dusting, much scrubbing and a list of other "muches" so she can present her home in showroom-fresh condition at all times on all occasions. Those very conveniences that have liberated her from mop, broom and scrubbing board, have bound her to sanitize, sterilize, deodorize and dehumanize her hospitality!

Paul exhorts us over and over again as Christians "to be given to hospitality"—Romans, 1 Timothy, Titus and 1 Peter. And we have Jesus saying, "Martha, Mary hath chosen the better part." So what's a poor woman to do?

We have Mary saying, "Don't count on me. I'm listening to the Word of God." And we have Martha holding the bag and saying, "Good grief!"

The answer is in balance, priorities and timing—all summed up in one word: flexibility. If Billy Graham's coming to dinner, I suggest you order cold cuts from the local deli and spend as much time listening to his conversation as possible. If it's Senator Stuffed-Shirt from Lower Slobbovia, you may welcome the opportunity of burying yourself in the beef roulade and having minimum time exposure to him.

My guests can always rate their congeniality by the time I spend with them. I favor more and more the open-kitchen policy where everyone comes in and out and helps sniff, taste or just sits and strums on their ol' banjo. Just call me Dinah!

Over the years I have been housebroken from the idiosyncrasies of prestige entertaining by a series of hilarious put-downs that have left me with the memory of warm or roaring laughter and not an ounce of dignity! Like the Christmas we had 40 guests in and the cesspool overflowed. Or the church New Year's Eve potluck for 65—for which I had spent the whole day in frenzied cleaning and tidying up. After a successful evening of gracious entertaining, I went into the bathroom and found I had left an unmentionable undergarment displayed over the shower rail.

Spic and Span was once my middle name. When I went through the Immigration Department for my American citizenship papers the clerk couldn't get a set of decent fingerprints. "You have Ajax fingers," she said. "The cleanser has worn away your fingerprints!" I thought of offering my services to the FBI as an undercover agent, but that was before Watergate.

Our flexibilities must always assure that our first priority is the witness of Christ and work of the Holy Spirit, even under the most inconvenient circumstances. One of the busiest days of my life was on the occasion my husband and I were committed to preparing a Japanese dinner for 150-plus guests at the little Episcopal church school where our children attended. For weeks I had cooked and frozen chicken teriyaki, stashing it into all the available neighborhood freezers.

When the great day arrived I had 350 pieces of teriyaki chicken thawing in my kitchen. We smelt like a soy sauce factory. In addition the dining-room table was littered with cucumber salad and pots of rice were steaming on the kitchen stove.

It was a sweltering hot California summer day and, as my car pulled out of the driveway to deliver the children for a quick dip in the local pool, I noticed a man sitting cross-legged in the bush area that buffers our home from the street. "Please, dear God," I muttered, "Not today. Don't land a hippie on my doorstep today. Look how much I've got to do. I just can't help anyone today!"

"Oh?" whispered my inner voice.

"Please, dear Lord, let him be gone by the time I get back!"

"Oh?" whispered my inner voice.

I could hear his chanting by the time I rounded the bend in the road. Not only was he still there, he was walking around the bushes with his arms upraised chanting. I slammed the door to the kitchen and thought of five reasons why I should either ignore him or get him arrested:

1. He was probably spaced out on drugs.
2. It was not safe for a woman alone in a house to strike up a conversation with a man in her bushes.
3. I should call the police and report him for trespassing.
4. My commitment for the day was to the dinner.
5. My husband would back me up in all the previous four.

Yet my mind kept repeating over and over again, "I was thirsty, and you gave me drink: I was hungry and you fed me" (see Matt. 25:35). Ah, that was it! Here I sat with 350 pieces of teriyaki chicken. I could feed 20 hungry hippies and not miss a piece. No wonder the Lord had brought him today. Today of all days was I ever prepared.

Triumphantly, I walked out to the garden gate. "Hello down here. Are you hungry?"

"Yes," came the shouted response, "I am."

"Stay where you are," I shouted back, "I'll bring you something to eat."

I warmed up five pieces of chicken, added some steaming rice, poured a glass of milk and moved out on my errand of mercy. I handed him the plate.

He took one look at the chicken and said, "Oh, I'm a *vegetarian!*" Three hundred and fifty pieces of chicken and this guy's a vegetarian.

I slunk back to the kitchen and switched the chicken for cucumber salad.

"What's your name?" I asked.

HAVE YOU EVER TRIED FEEDING CHICKEN
TO A VEGETARIAN?

"Tom," he said.

"Tom, I'm giving you this in the name of Jesus Christ. When you're done just throw the paper plate and cup into the trash bin." (And for heaven's sake move along, I thought!)

Two hours later he was still there. Three hours later he was still there. In between rushed trips of delivering chicken, rice and salad to the school hall, I'd wave and smile weakly at him.

Eventually I couldn't stand it any longer and got on the phone to a Christian brother in the canyon. When in doubt and especially when rushed and in doubt, pass the buck is my motto! One plants the seed, another waters after all.

Dick picked him up in his camper and he spent the night with the Grangers in the canyon. He had the witness of Christ in his belly and he had the witness of Christ in their kindness, testimony and hospitality of the evening. He did not make a commitment to Jesus, and he moved along the following morning.

We still hold him in prayer. It was only ours to give the "cup of cold water in My Name" (see Matt. 10:42). Our hospitality must be given, God chooses the time and tests the commitment.

Conversely, one of the most difficult things I've ever had to do was to refuse food to a pair of hungry men. They had just been released from prison and were "living" in the hills behind the Sierra Madre Canyon dam. Freedom, they called it—no shelter, but they got water from garden hoses and had wild cacti to eat.

I'd known them for over a year under many diverse circumstances so they knocked on my door. "Fay, we've got the trots and need something to eat." I brought them each a peanut butter and jelly sandwich and a glass of milk.

The next day, "Fay, we're still eating cactus and still have the trots, will you give us something to eat?"

"Why don't you go on down to the Rescue Mission; you can't go on like this. Or go to the Foothill Free Clinic, Salvation Army or one of the organizations that will help you rehabilitate?"

"No, we want to be *free!*"

"*Free?*" I replied. "You call this being *free?* Why you're in prison right now. You're in bondage to your very guts!" They did not respond and I gave them a tuna sandwich and a glass of milk.

The next day they were back looking more wasted than ever. "Please, Fay another sandwich."

I had spent much time the night before praying for them. I was not helping them. I was only hindering their eventual, but necessary decision. "No," I replied, "I am doing you a disservice by feeding you. You cannot go on this way, you must turn yourselves in to the authorities and get the medical and other help they can give you."

"Boy, Fay, you've changed, you've become hard. What's the matter with you?"

"No," I replied, "You must go for help. There are many organizations that will help you," and I once again named them off. "God bless you. I am praying for you."

I closed my door, went into the bedroom and wept. It was the first and only time I have ever refused food to anyone.

The Case for Sloth

A woman loves her annual medical checkup. There is always the chance that her deepest hypochondriac suspicion may be confirmed and she can go home clothed in the full regalia of martyrdom, turn accusingly on her husband and family with "I told you so. And all this time you've been dragging me out in the mornings to make your breakfast!"

"How nice to see you, Mrs. Angus, and how are you today?"

"Well, I think I've got diabetes, a low-grade mononucleosis, the possibility of a brain tumor and a bad case of dandruff."

"Aha," said the nurse, "we'll just mark you down as 'fatal' and send you to the morgue!"

Now Dr. Bill Gannon is the man through whose

hands my children were ushered into life, the man who etched his signature in the scar across my anatomy and the man who held my life in the beige manila file folder marked A-76. We had watched the wrinkles develop on each other's faces for 14 years. But the authoritative glare of his blue eyes always meant, "Cut out the funny stuff, and let's get down to business!"

The closest we'd ever got to an intimate conversation was during the breech delivery of my son when I groaned, "I think I'm dying," and he patted my hand and said, "There, there now, everything's going to be all right!"

Only once did I try to defy him. With a toss of my head I had said "Doctor, you are talking to a former ballet dancer, my endurance is excellent."

He had shot back, "And you, young woman, are talking to a former bronco buster. Do exactly as I say!"

So, here I was again for another annual checkup. The doctor asked, "How long is it since you've had your eyes examined?"

"Fifteen years," the exact length of my marriage. Frankly, I've been frightened to get new glasses in case a more thorough look at John will reveal he's not the man I thought I married. Furthermore the bathroom mirror now tells me through my myopic mysteria that I'm a cross between Sophia Loren and Audrey Hepburn, and who wants to change that!

Gannon knit his brows together. Doctors never wink or grin, they just knit their brows together—a trick taught them in medical school to give them an air of profundity when they're actually wondering whether they remembered to book themselves into the golf course for Tuesday morning. He said "What are your symptoms?"

The symptoms were inertia, the diagnosis was mental

fatigue and the prescription was *exercise!*

A dancer's body is the finest-tuned instrument in the world. So my decision to turn to flab was no accident. It was deliberately calculated after some 12 years of the excruciating vigor of classical ballet. The dance student's muscles are in a perpetual stretch position and her ramrod body is solid steel. This condition needs the maintenance of a minimum two hours grueling practice daily. The slightest relaxation of a dancer's rib cage means a poke from the *directeur* and the comment, "You're sagging, honey!"

The challenge of the dance is unending. If you do five pirouettes, you need to strive for eight. If you jump "so high" in your *grande jeté*, you need to try for even more elevation. The only motivation necessary is the accolade of achievement.

Part of the "I do's" of our marriage was John's insistence on my saying "I don't" to ballet. It was either or. He refused to share me with the limelight of the spotlight. I chose the "either" and have never regretted the "or," which resulted in my deliverance from an addiction to the *plié*.

For years after I stopped dancing my muscles would ache to be used. So I'd joyfully languish poolside and casually stretch out an arabesque now and then or do 15 *entrechats* on the way down from the diving board. But my daily exercise consisted only of washing out the ring around the bathtub.

It didn't take me long to soften up. I'd thumb my nose at my vigorous friends and settle in to the soothing noise of the rattle of the typewriter—my new means of expression.

Now Gannon was saying, "Tennis?"

I said, "No!"

"Swimming?"

70

"Occasionally!"

"Jogging?"

"Never!"

He then said "Walking, and that's an order!"

I said nothing.

Our negotiations boiled down to my promising to do five knee bends before I brushed my teeth and five knee bends after I brushed my teeth, with a set of ten alternate leg swings while waiting for the tea to steep. He said that would be fine as long as I brushed my teeth at least three times a day and drank lots of tea.

The unfortunate fact is that I've kept my promise, but I haven't brushed my teeth in two weeks, and I've switched to coffee. After all you never know when a knee bend might lead to a thrombosis, and one shouldn't take chances, should one?

The ultimate of any woman's lib cause is a day in bed when you're perfectly well. I don't get sick. I rejected the whole idea of getting sick after a childhood of pampering through bronchitis, pneumonia, inhalations of Friar's Balsam, a tonsillectomy and an appendectomy! And I had what you'd call an average adolescence—chicken pox and measles right on cue.

Part of my parental rebellion in my late teens was to stay perfectly well, to the tremendous frustration of a doting mother! I'm tired, draggy, cranky, half blind and woozy, but in excellent health.

Once in a while I take the luxury of a day in bed as my just due for never getting the flu. It's also my revenge for nursing everyone else through it! It's delicious to snuggle down deep into the covers, look through the window (that needs cleaning) at the brilliant California sunshine and the camellias in full bloom in late January, hear the birds singing and say "Ha! I'm staying right here!"

The kids come home from school. "Mom! Are you sick."

I snort, "Of course not!"

"Why are you in bed?"

"Because I want to be," with defiance.

"What's for dinner?"

"Nothing."

Whisper, whisper. "She's gone bananas. Wait 'til dad gets home!"

"Hiya, honey! What's the matter? You not feeling well?"

Snort. "No—I'm perfectly all right!"

"Why y' in bed?"

"Because I want to be!" That shook him up.

"Hum-m-m," says John. Then "hum-m-m," more profoundly as he walked out of the room. As I tiptoed past the kitchen door on the pretext of going to the bathroom, I heard such words as "Exercise . . . tired blood . . . we'll have to do something about it."

That Christmas I got a secondhand belt massage machine, bought by my daughter at a neighborhood garage sale; a rope pulley body conditioner guaranteed to restore any waistline—if hooked up to the bedpost and used five minutes a day (so far all it's done is wear a groove around the bedpost); and a book on cellulite. The toe of my stocking was filled with a bottle of Geritol.

Moreover, the after-dinner sport suddenly became "walking the mom!" Other families are content to walk their dogs, but not ours. The conspiracy was hatched with the casual remark "Let's go for a stroll around the block!"

It was a balmy evening so, arm in arm, we set off. Soon I was linked not only onto the arm of my long-legged husband, but on the other side onto the arm of my long-legged daughter. The stride picked up. Before

THE ULTIMATE IN WOMEN'S LIB IS A DAY
IN BED WHEN YOU'RE PERFECTLY WELL!

long I was huffing and puffing, doing two paces to their one and had to be dragged the final 50 yards back into the driveway.

The next night my son used a more direct approach. "Mom, I'm taking you for a walk!"

"Why?" I asked.

For an answer he thrust a copy of the *System Bible Study* (1938 Edition) under my nose, turned to the back to a section called "Character Building" and ran his grubby little finger along the lines: "Health depends on digestion, digestion depends on blood, the quality of blood depends on the circulation, and the circulation of the blood depends on exercise," and "Energy moves us to continuous effort; it fires the mind, soul and body with consuming passion for big things, great things— things that endure and bless mankind. If, in your soul, energy and enthusiasm are not wed, it is doubtful that your blessings will be 'counted one by one.' "

It is amazing how we find enthusiastic energy for those activities we enjoy, but sudden lethargy in the daily commonplace ritual of our lives. Still, productive energy is the alternative to sloth and it's a lot more fun!

The Bible has a lot to say about sloth, mainly "Be not—!" Jesus said, "Be not—!" Paul said, "Be not—!" Solomon said, "Be not—!" A real triptych of authority against laziness. Sloth has no place in the Christian life. Indeed, we are told to "redeem the time" (Col. 4:5), be productive.

One key to productivity is anticipation—having something to look forward to. Frequently when the children go off to school in the morning they ask, "Mom, what have I got to look forward to when I get home this afternoon?"

We check the calendar and if there's nothing there, noting a trace of the doldrums I say, "I'll plan a surprise!" They set off immediately with a spring in their step and burst back at the end of their day with a "What is it?" It's generally something very small—a magazine they've wanted, a fresh batch of cookies, occasionally a treasure hunt where they follow a trail of paper clues to a secret cache that may just hold a couple of candy bars! But it's enough to lift their spirits.

The adult is really no different. Goals and directives placed in a life will motivate it to active fulfillment. If there is a something-I've-always-wanted-to-do in your life, now is the time to prayerfully submit it before God the Father, ask the guidance of the Holy Spirit and then do it. Procrastination is the sin of "I have left undone those things which I ought to have done" (Matt. 23:23, paraphrased).

Cheer Up and Stand!

As we bang our drums, clang our cymbals and stand up and cheer Old Glory every fourth of July, let's remember that the message of St. Paul to the church is *Cheer up and stand!* It comes by way of our founding fathers in Rome, Corinth, Galatia, Ephesus, Philippi, Colosse, Thessalonica, and a youngster called Timothy.

Indeed there are nine exhortations to *rejoice*, balanced by nine exhortations to *stand* (usually fast in the faith) throughout the Pauline epistles; all this in the midst of shipwrecks, imprisonments, snake bites, lashings and the persistent nag of a thorn in his flesh that would make anyone else want to break down and quit rather than cheer up and stand. Not only did Paul stand but he ran a good race and fought a good fight while

77

living through the most traumatic period in the history of the Christian church.

If you're depressed by the state of the nation, or if you're depressed by the state of the world, take a long leap back into Paul's world. The Roman Empire was steeped in perversion and debauchery that was soon to lead to the wholesale martyrdom of Christians in the Colosseum. The decadence of Athenian temples was complete with human sacrifice.

"Cheer up," says Paul, not once in a while, but "always." Rejoice in the truth, rejoice in the hope and, (Phil. 3:1) "Finally, my brethren, rejoice IN THE LORD!" Rejoice in the exhilarating joy of the knowledge that it is in God we trust.

Were we to present Jesus with a penny in our day as did the Pharisees in their day (see Matt. 22:17–21), I could hear Him say, "And what saith this inscription?" Then with a twinkle in His eye, "Render unto God the things that are God's!" The least of those things is our coinage, the totality of those things is ourselves. America's strength was forged on the inscription "In God we trust."

In 1776 the great British statesman William Pitt said: "America is obstinate! America is almost in open rebellion! Sir, I rejoice that America has resisted. Three millions of people so dead to all the feelings of liberty as voluntarily to submit to be slaves would have been fit instruments to make slaves of the rest."

So help them God, America fought and won and raised up a standard that has led the world in life, liberty and the pursuit of happiness, the core of which is that all men are *created* equal—not evolved equal, not made equal, but *created* equal. In God, our *Creator*, we trust!

Anyone testifying in our courts of law is sworn "to tell the truth, the whole truth and nothing but the truth, *so help me God."* There are those undermining the spiritual constitutionality of our country who would rather swear "so help me *somebody!*" Or, "so help me *anybody*" or, "so help me *everybody!*" From whence cometh your help?

The *noblesse oblige* of our knowledge of God lies in active response. Where "ignorance is bliss," knowledge breeds responsibility. Herein Paul bids us *stand!* We glibly sing "Standing on the promises of God," then sit down on our spiritual haunches and ignore them. But don't only stand on them, appropriate them. I hold God to His promises.

When he was seven years old my young son Ian once confronted me at the dinner table: "Mom, there is something God can't do!"

"Mud in your eye," I said. "Never!"

"Wanna bet?"

"I don't bet and neither do you," I replied.

He had his parental lioness by the tail and he was enjoying every moment of it.

"OK, OK," I capitulated, "What can't God do?"

"Break His promises," he shouted!

He was right. Stand on them and claim them.

Four times Paul tells us to *stand fast:* "Stand fast in the faith" (1 Cor. 16:13); "Stand fast in the liberty wherewith Christ has set you free" (See Gal. 5:1); "Stand fast in one spirit" (Phil. 1:27); "Stand fast in the Lord" (Phil. 4:1; 1 Thess. 3:8). I usually stand slow, but I'm getting faster!

E pluribus unum—united we *stand.* Divided we usually build another church and that's not always bad. We're still "one body, and one Spirit, . . . one hope, one Lord, one faith, one baptism, one God and Father of all, who is above all, and through all, and in you all" (Eph. 4:4–6). We're just living in different sanctuaries. I never

79

get ruffled over all the hoo-haw of a church split. Sometimes a church split is a healthy sign, it at least shows that people are thinking for themselves.

Our own church is the result of a split way back when. The church we split from is just around the corner and both our pastors are the best of friends (now, that is—the pastors at the time of the split probably weren't), and alternate pulpits for Good Friday services, etc. Both churches are growing by leaps and bounds with overflowing attendance at double Sunday morning services. Just what they would have done if they hadn't split, from a pure accommodation standpoint, would have probably been to construct a new facility the size of the Mormon Tabernacle!

Cheers for denominationalism! It's the result of basic differences in the personality and related projected expressions of man. He needs the variables of the choices of worship. Hand-clapping fundamentalism may be very offensive to the liturgical nature of a man who worships best in the quiet refinement of the high Episcopal church. It does not mean that any one form is more spiritual than the other.

Denominationalism does not have to be the cause of disunity. Argumentative denominationalism is what's so abortive to Christian unity!

Our family is part of an interdenominational Christian community church that is a marvelous witness to the workability of a New Testament fellowship in a modern environment. Many of us theologically disagree, but it doesn't interfere with our love for one another—and that's the difference.

When theologies become aggressively argumentative is when the problems start. In his "one body, one Spirit, one hope, one Lord, one faith, one baptism, one God and Father of all," Paul gives us seven basic spiritual constitutional unities upon which to *stand.* Choose then to stand on the freedom of your worship.

"*Stand fast* therefore in the liberty wherewith Christ hath made us free, and be not entangled again with the yoke of bondage" (Gal. 5:1, italics added). Freedom is generally best appreciated by those who have at sometime in their lives lost it. And how they bless those who restore it to them.

After two and a half years in a Japanese prison camp during World War II we were liberated by the American army—one lieutenant and two GIs; then a couple of days later by the British army—one captain, one aide and two stretcher-bearers! The fact that the total complement of the task force ate one meal with us and then all came down with dysentery and had to be nursed through the next week by the captives, lent its chuckle to the situation.

Nevertheless, our liberators they were, and in due time they did set us free. How we blessed them and how we thanked God that there were men in uniform willing to pursue freedom and justice for all.

Jesus did that too—unto death. *Stand fast* in His liberty and be not entangled in the bondage of sin, habit or thought that would spin its web to hold you prisoner.

Cheer up and *stand confident* in the Lord. Janet Carr, Miss California and runner-up in the Miss America contest, used as the thrust of her message "*American* ends with the words '*I can.*'" The Christian adds "*I can* through Christ who strengthens me."

Two phrases we won't tolerate in our home are "I can't," and "Why me?" We reverse them to "I can through Christ" (and often with a little help from mom and dad), and "Why not me?" (generally with no help from mom and dad). The "I can't" of my life most often is translated into "I can, if you will help me."

81

If the silent majority does not stand up and cheer for what they believe in, they will soon become the silenced minority. As Christians we must indeed *stand* and be counted. The world desperately needs the moral and spiritual values of Christian leadership. I thrill to hear from such organizations as Christians in Government and rejoice in men and women committed not only to their service in the Christian community but to their service in the general community.

When Billy Graham was asked if he would be willing to run for governmental office some years ago he said he was already representative of the highest authority of the universe and any other position would be a step down! He was absolutely right. His call as ambassador of Christ and evangel of His Kingdom is his full-time commitment. But there are those called by God to the responsibility of national leadership, and it is a thrilling, challenging call to serve not only your God but also your country.

If I permit myself to criticize a situation, I must then commit myself to do my utmost to try and change that situation. Both Abraham Lincoln and Hitler proved the power of the individual. When anyone tells me about the awful state of affairs of such and such, I ask, "And what do *you* intend to do about it?" There is something that everyone of us can do, even if it's just to write our congressman. Laws are written to be improved. Quit griping and improve them!

America is one of the few countries in the world today where an individual can *stand* and be counted without being knocked down! There are those who sit on the sidelines and jeer—there are those who sit on the sidelines and cheer. God wants us down on the field playing to win!

The Tender Gender

Amo, amas,
I love a lass,
She is sweet
She is tender
She is of the feminine gender!

So goes the ditty that helped teach us the conjugation of the latin verb *amo* "to love"!

Today's member of this feminine gender says "To love—yeah, but how?" And in response she finds herself bombarded on all fronts and a few rears with manuals thrusting the superlatives of "fascinating," "fulfilled," "total," "liberated," "emerging," "transitional,"—plus a few more—to punctuate the psyche of her own God-given personality and transform her into a stereotype sensual performer that any thinking man can find in the pages of her current reading!

Indeed, "woman" has become the most copyrighted word in today's literary market. Intellectually and sensually ignored for generations, the spiritual woman has suddenly sensationalized her urges, and connubial capers are the topic of her day. Through all the ballyhoo there is a measure of merit, but it is a minimal measure of merit. And it in no way counterbalances the dangers of overemphasizing the necessity of sexual performance as the nirvana of marital bliss.

"Fay, phone your husband, midweek, in the afternoon, at the office, and tell him you crave his body."

I phoned my husband, midweek, in the afternoon, in the office—

"Yes?" came his familiar voice.

The pulse of a man's emotional status quo may be taken in the way he answers his business phone. A cheery "hello" means everything is well on Mount Olympus; "Angus speaking," means hurry up and get it over with. And a curt "yes?" means the blood pressure's rising, and he's very busily involved in the trivia of earning your living.

I missed his usual friendly "hello," and with more frivolity than sense, proceeded. "Hello darling." Then dropping my pitch a sultry two octaves lower, I whispered, "I just wanted you to know *I crave your body!*"

There was a long silence, followed by guttural, strangled sounds, followed by another long silence.

What he finally said is private, and ... unprintable!

My husband is a civil engineer. His mind functions on a slide-rule scale and, if I'm smart, I see to it that I carefully calculate to stay out of his calculus! He does not need me to crave his body at 3:00 in the afternoon

"HELLO DARLING... I CRAVE YOUR BODY!"

in the middle of a project-planning conference. Multiply my call by 30,000 other women who decided to follow the same suggestion the same afternoon, and you'll realize the real reason for the terrible state of our economy.

When John came home that evening I did not think it timely to try greeting him at the door in baby-doll pajamas and go-go boots. Instead I tacked up a sign on the door that read "Moved to Siberia, no forwarding address!"

The tragedy is that our focus has now become distorted and we have reached a saturation point of sensuality, self-analysis and the desire for personal fulfillment. Women, in particular, spend lifetimes in a search for self-identity and gratification instead of getting on with the job of productive living.

Women are confused, young women and old women. Patented, copyrighted boudoir behavior is breeding a generation of middle-aged courtesans with seduction as their middle name. Heaven help the harried husband who suddenly finds himself the center of a marriage manipulation. The women men like to "play" with are seldom the women men like to stay with—not many wives were lifted out of the brothel.

We need to reactivate the performance of words like "lady," "poise," "dignity," "wit," "good manners," "good taste" and "common sense," all of which have their appendant stimulating frivolities. Modesty is still a virtue and in spite of the startling national statistics, chastity has not gone out of style.

William Carey had engraved in his wife's wedding band: "One for the other, and both for God." Somewhere along the line we've left off the "both for God," looking only one to the other. It is not within the power of man and woman to totally fulfill each other. Our capability is only partial at best, however excellent that partial may be. History and literature are full of examples of romances that soured due to overexposure—the tensions of familiarity.

It is only when one takes the broader dimensions of life commitments and goals that our sensual and interpersonal balances are put in perspective and stabilized. Mutual respect and encouragement to develop the God-given gifts and directives in our lives, as well as the enjoyment of our own individual personality traits, are the ties that bind. How beautiful is the love that has endured despite all. Despite disease? Yes! Despite impotence? Yes!

Shakespeare wrote:
"Love is not love which alters
when it alteration finds
Or bends with the remover to remove:
O, no! it is an ever-fixed mark
That looks on tempests and is never shaken."
St. Paul says the same thing in Ephesians chapter 5.

Even as the world is making its analysis of the Women's Liberation Movement, so is the Church making its analysis of the woman in the pew. As never before we need to be spiritually equipped to prove our credibility and to respond to the challenges and opportunities now opening up to us.

The credentials of the Christian woman rise from the base of her obedient commitment to her faith, to the variables of remaining flexible to the call of God in her life. Individual analysis of a status quo, rather than stoic generalization to a traditional mold, is a good result of the marriage of psychology to theology. What's good for Jane may be devastating for Joan. Same with Joe and Jim!

Fortunately our pulpits are sensitized to the needs of the *individual* in the pew. And the ministry of personal

Christian counseling is becoming increasingly vital throughout our churches.

The majority of Christian women are called to be housewives. I use the term "housewives" deliberately, as I personally believe it embodies the greatest liberty for the American woman. An efficient, disciplined American housewife should have more time to call her own than a woman in any other occupation. Certainly, her hands may be busy but her mind is her own to think her thoughts and to fill with input of her own choosing; choosing that can range from her own original creativity, to television, to radio, to cassette tapes, to books (reading them or writing them!), etc. For the spiritual woman this time avails an opportunity for prayer, meditation, study and service.

I've probably got one of the wettest Bibles in Christendom! I'm forever flipping its pages with dripping dishpan hands while following along a cassette study tape. Once I got so engrossed in a message by Ian Thomas that I took the cassette player into the bathroom and balanced my Bible on the edge of the tub while I bathed. The Bible fell in for a literary baptism. Matthew, Mark, Luke and John didn't mind; however, I think Ian Thomas might blush to think he was speaking to me under such personal circumstances!

I've never found it necessary to go into a garret and close myself off from the rest of the world in order to meditate—I find meditating very rewarding while dusting the living room knickknacks, or reflecting very stimulating while listening to the background hum-m-m of the vacuum.

For years I was employed as an executive secretary and was paid to carry out someone else's thoughts. I find it delightfully refreshing to now have the time and liberty to think and carry out my own! Admittedly, there have been times when my husband has considered paying me *not* to carry out my own thoughts! His admonition to the family is very simply, "Everybody is entitled to think what he wants around here as long as he doesn't act on it!"

After the indulgence of a colonial childhood with a houseful of servants including my own personal amah (I never so much as combed my own hair until I was 12, much less wash out the ring from around the bathtub!), my adjustment to the American life-style of being cook, boy, coolie and amah to the family built in many resentments. It was Mahatma Gandhi who taught me the value of work and the honor of each man doing his own work. Ever since then I have considered housewifery a noble calling. Strangely I have found that it takes more time and energy to sit and grumble about work than it does to do it. I've learned to time jobs and can schedule accordingly—to wit, ten spare minutes means a bathroom adequately cleaned; half an hour, the living room and hall vacuumed; so on and so forth.

Call yourself a homemaker if you like but please call me a *housewife.* Be they ever so humble, some homes are pretty crummy! For two and a half years my family "home" was a five-foot by six-foot allotment of space in a woman's dorm in a prison camp. After the war, as my parents and I picked up the pieces of our shattered lives, our "home" was diggin's (rooms) with a shared bath and closet kitchen. Then early marriage took my new husband and me to an apartment-type complex with TVs and radios blaring while John tried to study for his professional-engineer's exam.

At last God has given us a house, and how I thank Him for it! That's the *house* part of the *housewife* that I like. The *wife* part is my vivid recollection of the first time John introduced me as his "wife!" I felt woozy all over and it was rather nice. I like being a *wife*, so please, call me a *housewife*.

An old cookbook I dug up at an estate sale was dedicated to the "plucky housewives of 1876 who master their work instead of letting their work master them!" Still true today. So get on the ball, Gertie! There is no valid reason for the "bored housewife syndrome." To every woman, the world offers stimuli on all fronts— sports, art, community service; and to the spiritual woman endless opportunities of Christian service unto her Lord.

Some women are called to careers, and the best interest of themselves and their families are served by their development in their field of endeavor. How I thank God for Madame Curie who stood with her husband to develop radium. For our women doctors, teachers, lawyers, artists and, yes, our receptionists, secretaries, clerks and bus drivers—from cafeterias to congress—if you are called to serve, serve well.

On the home front the quality of time spent with the family takes precedence over the quantity. The tragedy of the battered child bears witness to the fact that some women are totally incapable of caring for their children. So does the indolent selfishness that tunes in the TV for endless hours and pushes toddlers away and out. Phone calls, coffee-fests and time abusers keep the woman in the home and with the children but under circumstances that would do the child more good if indeed the mother were removed from the home and adequate child care arranged!

One of the happiest households I know is one where both parents work—they are teachers. They have five children ranging in age from 10 to 18. Duties are divided, not always executed correctly but most times adequately, and the conditions of the home are qualitative.

If you're called to work, develop the quality of your limited time with your family.

Splashed across the cover of a recent periodical was the statement "The American woman—On the move, but where?" The spiritual woman knows exactly where! Stepping out in the confidence of her identity within the Godhead, she moves according to the direction, opportunities and challenges He puts into her life. The world desperately needs the integrity and spiritual values of the Christian woman—let's give it that!

In 1898 when Eleanor Roosevelt returned to the United States from her schooling in England, she was told by her headmistress: "Be everything you can. Be everything you're capable of being."

So should we.

Simon Sez

The question that exploded into human destiny, changed the course of history and will continue to reverberate throughout theologies until kingdom come, is found in Matthew 16. It has become the pivot of our faith. Try as he may to circumvent all ideology and truth man cannot avoid the confrontation of Jesus to Simon Peter—simply, "But whom say ye that I am?" (Matt. 16:15).

The genesis of spiritual awakening and dawn of immortality lies in our response to the "whom" of the Christ. Where we came from and how we got here is no weight of balance to where we are going—the *quo vadis* of our life.

If I had but one question to ask the world, this is it. And if I had but one answer to give, I could only echo

Peter, "Thou art the Christ, the Son of the living God" (Matt. 16:16). The core of our commitment is then reinforced by Jesus, "Blessed art thou, Simon Bar-jona: for flesh and blood hath not revealed it unto thee, but my Father which is in heaven. And I say unto thee, That thou art Peter, and upon this rock—upon you and your statement of faith—I will build ... I will *build* ... I will BUILD my church—my people, my called out ones, my ecclesia; and the gates of hell shall not prevail against it (them)" (Matt. 16:17,18 paraphrased). Jesus BUILDS upon our response to Him.

Mrs. Billy Graham says that on her tombstone she wants a road sign "Construction completed, thank you for your patience!"

Simon goes on and sez a couple of crummy things like his rebuke to Christ "Be it far from thee, Lord: this shall not be unto thee" (Matt. 16:22), and his triple denial in Matthew 26:69–74. Fortunately he got over all this, after being called Satan once and being brought to his senses by the crowing of a rooster. He then went on and sez a whole lot more in his two epistles, called 1 and 2 Peter instead of 1 and 2 Simon.

The *statement* of our faith in Jesus as Lord, the *appropriation* of that faith when we believe in our heart and confess with our mouth (see Rom. 10:9) and the *commitment* of our life to the belief—that equates to one obligation—*obedience*, unmitigated obedience. Obedience is the mortar with which we build the Christian life: "If a man love me he will keep [obey] my words" (John 14:23).

Ours is a non-negotiable faith. Too often we live in a state of spiritual detente, compromising our commitment, which limits the effectual flow of God's will in our lives. Too often we practice the "*if you* will ... *then I* will"—politics in our prayers rather than the unconditional obedience that puts us in gear to move out under the thrust of the guidance of the Holy Spirit in our lives. Simon Peter sez, "Elect, according to the foreknowledge of God the Father, through sanctification of the Spirit, *unto obedience*" (1 Pet. 1:2, italics added).

A year ago a neighborhood accident placed a little five-year-old girl in the intensive care unit of our local hospital. As she fought for her life for several days her young Christian father prayed, "O God, if you spare Crissy and save her life I will give you my whole life." A political negotiation!

The impact hit him as he looked in the mirror while shaving the next morning and God spoke directly and positively to him, "What if I don't spare her?" Immediately he knew the question was not Christine's life, but his own obedience. Once again he fell to his knees. "No, O God, whether you spare Crissy or not, my life is yours!" Unconditional commitment, the foundation for the building of our faith.

Some years ago I met a brilliant pathologist. Over coffee one evening I asked him, "Doctor, what is the purpose of your life?" Now here was a man deeply involved in saving human life. The pathology lab is the control center of a hospital. The surgeon's knife moves according to the yea or the nay of the biopsy or lab findings. It is life-and-death drama on a day-and-night basis. As diseased tissue is rushed from surgery and the operation put on hold, the pathologist makes his quick analysis—take off the breast, the leg; or take out the colon, or spare it!

I fully expected the doctor to reply, "Find a cure for cancer" or "Alleviate human suffering" or to indulge in some other medical history-making aspiration. He and his wife, a qualified doctor in her own right, are a team surely committed to medicine! However, without a moment's hesitation his black eyes found mine and he said, "The purpose of my life is to *glorify God.*"

Glorify God? Glorify God! His simple answer whipped my soul and turned my life. My call to obedience to "glorify God in [my] body and in [my] spirit, which are God's" (1 Cor. 6:20).

At that time I was broadcasting a monthly radio program which was a most satisfying outlet for my own poetry and that of other writers in the area. I loved mingling with sensitive, creative people and welcomed the silent applause that came by way of letters or phone calls of tribute. Once a performer, always a performer! I had merely exchanged my ballet tutu for a sensual voice!

"And whom does it glorify?" asked my Lord. "Why me, of course," responded I.

The spiritual tug o'war on my ego had begun. Yes, I rationalized, "But Lord, I write spiritual poems—surely they glorify you!"

"Yea-h-h," said my heart. I had done my last broadcast. It was a call to obedience, retroactive a few weeks!

The pastor of a large Pasadena church graduated from Yale's theological school some years back. "Well, here I am," he thought, "launched forth with a good education behind me, all set to be a *successful* preacher."

God dealt with him up at Arrowhead Springs, "Bill, I didn't call you to be *successful,* I called you to be *faithful!*" Obedience, the keynote and turning point of his ministry!

As anchor man of the faith Simon Peter goes on to give us the authoritative formula for successful Christian living, "Give diligence to make your calling and election sure: for *if ye do these things, ye shall never fall*" (2 Pet. 1:10, italics added).

The building blocks for abundant knowledge of our

Lord Jesus Christ and additives for the fulfillment of our calling are stacked up in 2 Peter 1:5–7:

Add to your faith *virtue;*

and to virtue *knowledge;*

and to knowledge *temperance;*

and to temperance *patience;*

and to patience *godliness;*

and to godliness brotherly *kindness;*

and to brotherly kindness *charity.*

Seven victorious antidotes to knock out the seven deadly sins! Simon sez "do this, do this, do this, do this, do this, do this, do this (seven times) and you won't *do that!*"

Theology and
Other Trivia

Nothing rattles the skeleton of our faith more than a direct confrontation with theology. *Theo*, meaning "God," *logos* meaning "word," and the combination of the two meaning seminaries, provosts, deans and a long list of modern counterparts of the book of Leviticus.

The slogan of most theologians is "That's controversial!" Said with the right air of profundity it settles all arguments and leaves the parties to both sides of the question feeling compatible, if not with each other at least with the theologian. Unfortunately, the slogan of a few theologians is "If you can't convince 'em, confuse 'em!" Which is why we have Baptist seminaries, Lutheran seminaries, Jesuit seminaries, et al.

Theology is what divides the pulpit from the pew, and sometimes the first five pews from the next five pews.

Seeing as our family generally sits well back in about the twentieth pew on the right-hand side, occasionally hiding behind a pillar or two, we have developed the credo, "We'll try it, we might like it!" or "If it worked for you, it might work for me!"

Every true theologian must win his laurels through (1) publication and (2) the test of the adult Sunday School. It's the latter that gives him spiritual ulcers. In his seminary he is undisputed authority. But scaled down to a diagnostic analysis on the Sunday School level, he is definitely disputed authority. Sometimes he resolves the disputes and sometimes he provokes the disputes, depending on the state of his digestion.

Being territorially close to a large theological seminary, our church has been fortunate enough to draw on many of the school's wise men to teach our Sunday School class from time to time. Seeing as how this same seminary swiped our pastor a few years back to be their Dean of Homiletics, we feel it is only right that they replenish in kind. As a result we are rapidly developing into the only national Sunday School class with 65 lay theologians! This makes for a very rousing discussion period. Sometimes it's rousing to edification, but more often it's rousing to blood pressure, generally the teacher's.

I recall one Sunday morning, while enjoying a series on the book of Romans taught by Fuller's Provost Glenn Barker, a newcomer lay theologian collared me during the preliminary coffee time and asked, "Is he Calvinistic?"

"I dunno," I replied. "He's a terrific speaker, most helpful and besides, he's rather good looking, don't you think?"

Most women base their theology on those three points, not always in that order. Perhaps that's why

101

there are so few women theologians. One woman theologian who has fascinated me, after I got over the initial shock that her name meant "weasel," is Huldah the prophetess in 2 Kings 22:14. She dwelt in the college in Jerusalem, which makes me wonder if it was the first thrust towards a coeducational theological seminary. Something for the clerics to muddle over!

The gauge of your family's theology is the magnitude of your theological library. I have visited families who boast five shelves of theological books, Greek and Hebrew included, which always gives me a sinking feeling in the pit of my stomach. Our family's theological library consists of four copies of the Bible (one for each member of the family), Henrietta Mears' *What the Bible Is All About* and a dog-eared *Halley's Bible Handbook*. We also have an inherited copy of the *Confessions of St. Augustine*, which I dust off every once in a while but that I don't think any of us have read yet.

The man I admire most on a seminary campus is the Dean of Practical Theology. Actually, the man I would admire most, if ever I could find a seminary which had one, would be the Dean of *Impractical* Theology, because that's where most of my theological problems lie. It all begins with Proverbs 31——

Regularly, twice a year, the Christian woman is confronted with Proverbs 31—on Mother's Day and, for some inexplicable reason, on Father's Day. Maybe it's because fathers don't have a Proverbs 31 of their own extolling the virtuous man. Or maybe there's no such thing as a virtuous man so he has to look to the woman in his life for virtue. Who knows? Anyway at least twice a year—and sometimes far more frequently, such as at mother-daughter banquets when it's printed on the front page of the program, or on Valentine's Day when your husband tucks "Proverbs 31" into his bouquet of roses—

a woman is challenged to respond to this bit of theology. After 20 years of twice or thrice a year exposure, I resolved to grapple and come to terms with the virtuous woman.

"Her children arise up, and call her blessed" (v. 28), gave me the most trouble. Any mother will agree, getting her children to "arise up" at all every morning, much less call her "blessed," is a feat of great accomplishment. I've tried all slants.

"Good morning, Mary Sunshine, and how are you today?"

"Aw, come on, mom, five more minutes!"

"Time to rise and shine, little chicks. This is your blessed mother—"

"Knock it off, mom!"

"Awake, beloved, it is the dawn!" (from the *Rubaiyat of Omar Khayyam*, to appeal to their poetic subconscious).

"Shucks, mom, it's the middle of the night!"

The times my children most often call me blessed is from a prone position such as lying in the hammock when I bring them a cold glass of lemonade, or on a beach towel when I unpack a picnic, or during breakfast in bed on a Saturday morning. Getting your children to call you blessed is one thing; getting them to arise up is another and never the twain doth meet!

I score two out of four for clothing the household in scarlet (v. 21). Perhaps a little better if you can count a red decor kitchen as part of the household clothing! My daughter Twinkie and I love red and include lots of it in our wardrobes. But, as for the boys, the closest we can get to clothing them in scarlet is for them to condescend to a red sweater or vest at Christmas and a smattering of red tone ties on other occasions. I once bought my husband a modified scarlet shirt (pink) and it nearly cost me my marriage! If the name Angus conjures up a man in tweedy plus fours, argyle socks and a cashmere cardigan, you've got it right. And a pink shirt doesn't fit!

Bringing food in from afar (v. 14) is a lot easier since MacDonald's and Kentucky Fried Chicken came to town. I did rise up once when it was yet night (v. 15) and prepared not meat but, in this case, a rice pudding for the household, and with disastrous results. Battling with insomnia at 4:00 A.M. I decided that it was now or never to try out verse 15 on the family, and with what more virtuous a way than by a nice hot rice pudding for a breakfast change and treat!

With visions of bubbling pudding topped with raisins and laced with strawberry jam, I was breaking my eggs and beating my milk, humming a little hum unto the Lord, when the pans crashed down to the kitchen floor. Within seconds Ian was there, squint-eyed with his BB gun, falling over Zip the dog who had beat him to the kitchen by only a hair. John dashed in, pulling on a robe with one hand and fumbling with his glasses with the other, and Twinkie trailed in the rear yelling sleepily "Who's there?"

I smiled sheepishly, "Hi, you guys, I'm making a rice pudding for breakfast!"

Verse 15 is now marked in my Bible: "Forget, eliminate—dispensation granted!"

We bought a field once (v. 16) jointly; the heart of my husband doth not safely trust in me enough to permit any financial adventure without due consultation. It was supposed to triple in value and make us a fortune. That was 10 years ago. We still have the field and keep pouring more and more annual taxes into it with no return. It's too far away to planteth with a vineyard, and I don't think that the church would approve of our growing vintage grapes anyway.

However, one time we did plant a few vines of grape (table variety) in our backyard. But they shriveled up and died within six weeks!

My husband doth not sit among the elders of the land, and after Watergate I'm glad! He doth not even sit among the elders of the church. But he doth usher once in a while and spent six years leading a men's Bible study class—wherever that puts him in verse 22. If everyone's husband was an elder in the church, much less an elder in the land, it would be chaotic leadership with too many chiefs and no Indians!

He is an elder at the office, however, with more and more college graduates swarming in year after year. The first time his young engineers started calling him "Sir," he won his eldership diploma!

See what I mean about needing a Dean of Impractical Theology? Never mind, we may all flunk Proverbs 31. But if our husbands still call us "darling" after 15 years of marriage and our kids shout "Awright mom, you're OK!" every once in a while, it all adds up to a "*blessed*" or two!

A story with a lot of theological zap comes from the pulpit of Pastor Jim Hewett of Arcadia Presbyterian Church. He imagines a conversation between Jesus and His disciples in the boat as they cross the Sea of Galilee to the land of the Gadarenes. Mark, chapter 5:

"OK, Lord," says Peter, "we're all fired up and raring to go. What's our goal?"

"We will convert the 10 cities of the Decapolis," says Jesus.

"Ten cities?" cries Peter. "Why we don't have enough man power! If we go out two-by-two, we need at least eight more men."

"I have my plan, Peter," says Jesus.

"What's the strategy?" says Peter. "Are you going to

divide us up into teams and give us a couple of cities each?"

"No," says Jesus, "I don't plan on using any of you."

A long pause of dumbfounded silence as the disciples look around at each other.

"You're not going to use any of us?" says Peter. "After you've trained us all this time? Who are you going to use?"

"I've got my man," says Jesus.

"You've got your man? One man?" says Peter.

"Yup," says Jesus.

"Now let me get this straight," says Peter looking around at all the other disciples who are nodding their heads in agreement to urge him on. "We are going to convert 10 cities, you're not going to use any of us, your trained disciples, but you have one man going to do the job?"

"Yup," says Jesus.

"Boy, who is the man," says Peter. "Is he in seminary over there now? Who did he study with?"

"Well," says Jesus, "he hasn't gone to any seminary, and right now he's a raving lunatic running around naked in the tombs."

The criterion of Christian witness? The touch and call of Christ!

Functional Faith

Faith comes fully equipped with an instruction manual. Fit together all the easy-to-assemble, snap-on parts and you will have a completely functional, sturdy product. It's not made in Japan nor even in America, but in an omnipotent factory by the Master Craftsman. It is delivered not C.O.D. but completely free.

Faith comes in the basic color called "perfectly clear." But you are free to paint it up any way you like—conservative grey, flashy fuchsia, camouflage khaki or moderate brown. The only color it rejects is insipid whitewash. But whatever the colors, it can change them at will like a chameleon.

Fortunately, faith is washable. But unfortunately, it is also breakable, and if you try hard enough you can destroy it. However, it can be mended to look like new or even better than new. Even as scar tissue over a damaged heart is stronger than the original tissue, so mended faith is stronger than original faith.

It is a product with moving parts that need constant maintenance—oiling, grooming, touching up here and there. And like most products with moving parts it functions best when used regularly. Otherwise it can get rusty and squeak a lot. If not misused, it is guaranteed to last a lifetime.

It is very elastic and can be stretched and shared. As a matter of fact, the more you stretch it the more elastic it becomes. And as for sharing, people have been known to coast along for ages on someone else's faith before finally ordering their own personalized model.

What shape, form or dimension does faith have, you ask? Well, that's up to you. You can fit it together in whatever way you desire. Your faith may be slightly different than my faith. God doesn't mind. In fact He's delighted to see it in varying forms and colors, big or small, an evidence in the creativity of man.

Faith has been thoroughly tested and is endorsed by such scriptural celebrities as Honest Abe who, "when he was called to go out into a place which he should after receive for an inheritance, obeyed; and he went out, *not knowing whither he went*" (Heb. 11:8, italics added).

Daring Dan, through his faith, defied a king and found himself the *pièce de résistance* on the menu in a den of lions. However, after spending a nerve-shattering night in this predicament, he was able to say victoriously, "My God hath sent his angel, and hath shut the lions' mouths, that they have not hurt me" (Dan. 6:22).

Jittery Job was, according to God "a perfect and an upright man, one that feareth God, and escheweth evil" (Job 1:8). He had to writhe and wail around on an ash heap for 42 chapters, tormented by all the wiles of the

DANIEL FOUND HIMSELF ON THE MENU IN THE LION'S DEN, BUT...

devil to prove God's point, until his unwavering faith rang through with: "So the Lord blessed the latter end of Job more than his beginning: for he had fourteen thousand sheep, and six thousand camels, and a thousand yoke of oxen, and a thousand she asses. He had also seven sons and three daughters" (Job 42:12,13).

Enoch was translated and never saw death. Noah built his ark though he'd never seen rain. And Joshua marched his army around Jericho for seven days, which was a bit rough on the soldiers' feet. But by his faith the walls of the city fell down and the soldiers could then all sit down!

Moses, probably the most famous of all Old Testament scriptural celebrities, and whom Cecil B. De Mille and Charlton Heston went on to make even more famous, chose to "suffer affliction with the people of God, than to enjoy the pleasures of sin for a season" (Heb. 11:25). His choice resulted in the Ten Commandments, the Passover, the crossing of the Red Sea and other impressive faith-born miracles over 40 years of meanderings.

To give the ladies their due, there was Sarah, who had a baby when she was 90 (Gen. 17:17); Rahab the harlot (Josh. 2); and of course the most faithful of them all, Mary, the mother of Jesus.

How do you get faith?

Well, first of all you have to want it. Then you have to order it yourself—no party lines or stand-ins. All calls must be placed person-to-person.

There are various toll-free direct lines on all vibration levels. You can call J-OHN 3-16 or J-OHN 14-6. Or you can call R-EVEL-ATION 3-10 or numerous others, anytime, day or night, seven days a week, year in and year out.

You give your name, then say, *"I believe,"* and you'll

get immediate custom delivery there and then. If you're a bit shaky on the "I believe," you can say *"I believe, help thou my unbelief,"* and you'll still get delivery there and then. If by any chance you don't get immediate delivery, there is a customer service complaint department. You just call P-R-A-Y-E-R, say "Help me, Lord!" and that will set administration in motion to resolve your difficulties.

What you do with your faith after you get delivery is, of course, entirely up to you. You can dress it up or down, show it or hide it; you can even destroy it. You can add to it with more moving parts—call L-UKE 17:5. You can walk by it; you can stand in it; you can wash your heart with it; you can use it as a shield; you can be healed by it; you can overcome the world by it. You can even move mountains with it. Men have lived by it and men have died by it.

Faith has been known to subdue kingdoms, obtain promises, stop up the mouths of lions, quench violence, raise the dead and to be effectual in a series of episodes that would bring out a whole new edition of *Ripley's Believe It or Not!* And you'd better believe it, as we have on file documented evidence substantiating all the above claims.

Probably the most tangible testimony we have on file is that of John who states, "That ... which we have *heard*, which we have *seen* with our eyes, which we have *looked upon*, and our *hands have handled* ..." (1 John 1:1, italics added).

Faith is not blind, it sees and is seen. But the most awesome fact of all is that without faith we are unable to please God! (Heb. 11:6).

Adversaries and Advocates

Our house has been burglarized three times. Not the cloak-and-dagger, thief-in-the-night sort of thing, but plain old prime-time-broad-daylight breaking and entering. Twice windows were broken and this last time a panel was sawn out of the back door. Which all goes to show that when a guy wants in, he wants in!

Yes, we have a family dog, a friendly mutt who has shared so much in the "given to hospitality" of our home that no doubt he invited the burglars in and offered to make them a cup o' tea. The next dog we get will be a cross between a great dane and an elephant, and we'll name him Hitler to psyche him up for his duties on patrol. The only trouble is that, with our luck, he'll probably run out at the first sound of the bell like one of Pavlov's dogs, bite the Avon lady and we'll be slapped with a lawsuit for spilt lipsticks to the tune of $25,000.

We've learned a lot from burglars. I might even go into criminology—the study of, not the practice of, that is—in my old age. Burglars are very thorough, know exactly what they're looking for and are doubtless very quick. Each time, every cupboard and drawer was opened and systematically gone through. Those showing any signs of booty—like a small piece of jewelry or fifty cents in change—were dumped out on the floor for faster observation. Once, all our Christmas gifts were ripped open, and we felt rather insulted that none was stolen. Which goes to show the quality of our Christmas giving.

The police in our little town are getting to know us very well. We wave at each other every time a squad car passes at a local intersection. This might make bystanders think I work for the CIA or something dashing like that. But actually it's just a result of their growing intimacy with our family, our messy drawers, what I have in my lingerie cupboard and the somewhat embarrassing fact that, when they walked into my daughter's room, they gasped "Boy, they sure were thorough in here."

To which I had to blush and reply, "Oh no, officer, it always looks like this. I don't think they even bothered to come in here."

This now gives me liberty to lay down the law to the children with, "Pick up your rooms before you leave the house; do you want the burglars to think we live in a pigsty or something? And what will Officer Christensen think?"

Unfortunately, we have precocious children, and their response is, "Don't be silly, they never bother with our rooms. Why don't you just put your valuables under our messes? Then they'll be perfectly safe!"

The fact is, that after three burglaries, we don't have many valuables left. And what few valuables we do have are now safely deposited in the bank vault. Which is a good excuse for my husband to say in the middle of an elegant dinner party at a fancy restaurant, "Honey, you forgot to get your jewels out of the bank again."

Actually, he knows as well as I do I don't have any jewels worth beans to get out of the bank. But it makes for an excellent impression, especially when you've offended the waiter by asking for some ketchup for the *pâté de foie gras*.

I pick up the fantasy and say, "Yes, my diamond brooch would have looked lovely with this gown. What a shame! Ah well, that's the price of living in such a sinful society." The elegant dinner party conversation then revolves around who has been burglarized and who hasn't and, I'm sorry, but in today's set if your home hasn't been burglarized you just haven't arrived socially.

People are putting up signs that say "Beware of the Dog" when they don't even have a dog. They're getting alarm systems installed which their children are constantly tripping by mistake, bringing up three squad cars full of police with revolvers drawn, which the children love but the police don't. People are putting bars on their windows and finding themselves trapped inside and unable to escape in case of fire. And the bank vault business is booming.

We're thinking of solving the problem by pinning up a few signs of our own at all entries and exits:

This house has already been burglarized. I'm sorry but there's nothing of value left. Our few remaining jewels are at the bank and there is no money in the house. If you decide to come in anyway, please wipe your feet and leave

things nice and tidy for the police—we have
a reputation to uphold.

The unsavory fact of the matter is that crime is on the increase, from petty theft to grand larceny. And we'd better not underestimate the ingenuity of the criminal, whether in "high places" or right here in our own backyards.

One of the greatest tactical errors in warfare, criminal or military, is that of underestimating the enemy. During World War II, the famous American journalist Cecil Brown, in writing his cover story of the sinking of the British battleships *Prince of Wales* and *Repulse*, analyzed the tragedy by saying, "It's a mistake to underestimate the enemy. It seems to me the best thing is to figure the enemy is twice as good as you are and twice as smart, and then you make preparations in advance. . . . There is always the danger of underestimating the enemy to the point where you are overconfident."

He was perfectly right and wartime maneuvers have proven his statements over and over again. British Admiral Phillips and Captain Leach stood on the bridge of the *Prince of Wales* as she sank, waved and called out to their men "Good-bye, thank you, good luck and God bless you!" Two valiant men, together with countless others, went down with their ship.

Spiritual warfare is no different. Our adversaries are many, Paul calls them "principalities, powers, rulers of the darkness of this world"—and this is spooky—"not of flesh and blood!" (see Eph. 6:12). Peter gives one a name, "your adversary, the devil" (1 Pet. 5:8). Jesus called him the "prince of this world" (John 12:31; 14:30; 16:11). A formidable crew trained in the espionage of spiritual infiltration to seek out and attack the weaknesses of humankind.

Our strategy is to be sober (serious), vigilant and to resist on all fronts (see 1 Pet. 5:8,9). Our greatest vulnerability is to *underestimate* the enemy. We know him as a liar, a cheat and a deceiver. More and more I am finding him a thief, out to steal away the blessings of God in our lives—relationships, health, success—from our spiritual inheritance in Christ right down to the nitty-gritty practicalities of our daily life.

Has he stolen your self-confidence recently? Your faith? How about your joy? Wife? Husband? Children? These are all part of the blessings of God in our lives, they belong to us. Yet over and over again I see them sneaking out the door, burglarized by all the demonic forces of hell! Be aware of the ingenuity and strength of the enemy in your own spiritual backyard. And don't underestimate him.

One of the prize possessions for the spiritual thief, the diamond of jewels so to speak, is to steal away the glory of God. Throughout Holy Writ, in both the Old Testament and in the New Testament, in the terrestrial and in the celestial, the glory of God is manifest. He is glorified throughout the earth, He is glorified throughout the heavens and He is glorified in man through the indwelling presence of Christ—"Christ in you, the hope of glory" (Col. 1:27).

The glory belongs to God through Jesus Christ. It is not ours to give Him the glory, it's already His. It is only ours to steal away! Hence we should not pray "And I'll be sure to give You the glory," but rather "And I'll be sure not to steal away Your glory!"

Yet as spiritual thieves, we do steal His glory, time and time and time again. We seek to pit the endeavor and achievement of our own lives against the incomprehensible magnitude of His glory, the full dimensions of which we are unable to assimilate until we have indeed been translated and conformed to His image. It is not even within our puny power in our present state to see the fullness of His glory! It is a progressive revelation culminated in totality when we at last become one with Him!

"Resist the devil, and he will flee from you" (Jas. 4:7). Is the enemy stealing away your resistance?

I recently had a letter from a girl who was at the extremity of her endurance—two marriages on the rocks, several small children and then a year of serious illness. The valley of the shadow of life is at times more difficult to pass through than the valley of the shadow of death. But, in either case, David has given us the key in his use of the word "through" in Psalm 23.

Notice that the psalmist did not say, "Yea, though I live in the valley of the shadow of death." Rather, he said, "Yea, though I walk *through* the valley of the shadow of death [sometimes the valley of the shadow of life], I will fear no evil: for thou art with me; thy rod and thy staff they comfort me."

Satan would ambush us in that valley of the shadow, hold us there to pitch our tents and make it our dwelling place, our abode, our home. *Never!* Resist and keep walking *through*. For you won't get through unless you keep walking, staggering or even crawling at times!

Yes, keep moving forward! And remember, you are not alone. For God is with you. So just lean on Him as you are walking through the valley, and He'll lead you out.

We have many adversaries, but we also have an Advocate.

I've been to court with kids in trouble a few times and once or twice I've been able to act as advocate for them, pleading their case before the judge. In one instance as an advocate, I heard a so-called Christian kid, holding

119

his Bible, tell such whopping lies while on the stand that my own Bible became a red-hot branding iron in my hands. It was all I could do to keep from crying out! People do odd things in court.

When I took out my American citizenship papers, I had to have with me two advocates to swear that I was on the up and up and wouldn't drag my heels for Uncle Sam. How many times are we called upon to "put in a good word" for someone. Well, we have Someone, at the right hand of God the Father, the most influential position of all, to put in a good word for us. And He does! Read John 17 and you'll see firsthand all the good words He's already put in for us!

Not only do we have an Advocate in high places but we have an Advisor in low places, *vis-à-vis* dwelling within us—our own personal Central Intelligence Agency in the form of the Holy Spirit who gives us discernment, advice, and—when we blow the whole thing—"the Spirit also helpeth our infirmities" (Rom. 8:26).

Hanging in our entrance hall is an "Eye of God." It's hanging wrong side out, deliberately. Given to me some years ago by a young man in our canyon, Ron the Beadmaker, it's a beautiful piece of handiwork—colored yarn woven around crossed sticks with tassels hanging from its corners and a penetrating "eye" of blue and black yarn in the center. Tradition behind the fetish is that the colors are supposed to dilute all evil from entering the home and funnel it through the central eye (of God) to purify it and keep the home from harm.

Ron made these by the dozen, beautifully done in all colors and sold them at local art fairs. There was a time when practically every window in our canyon sported one. I was delighted with his gift.

"Oh Ron," I said, "this is just beautiful, I'll always

treasure it, but I hope you don't mind if I hang it inside out, because you see, that's where its real truth is displayed."

"Wha' d'ya mean?" he asked.

We turned it over, and there predominant was the cross around which the yarn was woven. "Here is my 'eye of God,' Ron," I said. "Not only my 'eye,' but my heart of God, my soul of God, my spirit of God and my body of God—the cross of Jesus Christ through which indeed all evil is dispelled!"

15

A Is for Author ——

When my first book was published and I presented a "hot-off-the-press" copy to the family at dinner, my husband said, "May I have a few words with you in the bedroom, dear?"

We excused ourselves to the stunned silence of the children and I thought, "Wow, this is going to be the love scene of all love scenes! He'll kiss me from the tips of my fingers to the—well, he'll kiss me, and it will be homage with a capital H!"

John shut the door, grasped me firmly by the shoulders with both hands, stooped down to look me straight in the eye and said, "I just want you to know that you may be the *author* in the family, but I am still the *author*-ity!"

Before I could catch my breath, our nine-year-old son

barged in shouting, "I need a lawyer," followed by a teary-eyed teenager whimpering, "You said I liked Alvin and the Chipmunks. I'll be the laughingstock of all my friends!"

My literary career was launched.

Being an author is going to bed at night with a pad, pencil and flashlight under your pillow in case you wake up at 2:00 A.M. with an inspiring thought. It's also pausing in the middle of a passionate embrace to say, "Can't you say something funny, I'm short two pages in my new chapter!"

Being an author is having your husband say "I love you" every night for the 17 years of your marriage and, after your publication, have him suddenly preface that statement with "You'd better let me see what you wrote today."

Being an author is responding to your husband's "I love you," with "That's plagiarism, can't you be more original?"

Being an author is having a pad and pencil on a string attached to a nail on the bathroom wall and having to read all the doodles recorded there by other members of the family under the heading "inspiring thoughts." And then forgetting to remove the pad and pencil when you have company and find not only have they read your family's intimate doodles but have recorded some of their own! Being an author is lying awake nights in fear that your publishers will get hold of said pad and pencil on a string, publish it and you and your family will then have to move to Lower Slobbovia.

Being an author is having your husband, your children, your mother, your mother-in-law, your aunts and cousins and especially the ladies in the sewing circle ask you "When are you going to think about your family?"

I think about my family every day, it's called "perish

the thought." But every June I close up my typewriter, put my brain on hold, zipper up and strap down all literary creativity, fortify myself with several cups of tea and settle down to thinking about my family nonstop throughout the summer vacation. What I think about them during that time is nobody's business (God knows and He forgives me often enough). It usually ends in September with dark circles under my eyes, three "hallelujahs" and one "Praise the Lord" that they're all back in school!

This past winter I was thrown a curve and had to stop and have an unscheduled "think" about the family during two weeks of the measles. At that time I could be found sitting trance-like on each of their beds, looking at them nonstop, with a thermometer in one hand and a cup of beef broth in the other, until they said, "For heaven's sake, stop thinking about us and go about your business."

"But what about my mother, my mother-in-law, my aunts and cousins and the ladies in the sewing circle?" I wailed. "You're ten years old. You'll soon be off to college, married, away from home, and I haven't thought about you enough!"

"Quit it," said Ian. "And stop staring at me like that. You look like a vulture!"

Being an author is worrying about getting your book done, then being sorry once it's done because you were looking forward to doing it.

Being an author is writing about keeping slim and trim while putting on seven pounds over the Christmas holidays—which makes you look pudgy and dumpy—and then being asked to speak to an assembly of 250 ladies, all of whom have read your book on keeping slim and trim. And then you try to take off the seven pounds in four days so that you won't look pudgy and dumpy to

"MOM, STOP STARING LIKE THAT. YOU LOOK LIKE A VULTURE!"

the 250 ladies who are expecting you to look slim and trim! After you've spoken to them you can then put on another seven pounds and look pudgy and dumpy again until the next public appearance.

Being an author is meeting a guy in the supermarket who bought four of your books at a recent autograph party. You have your hair in curlers and are wearing your torn jeans. And you try to look incognito when you see that glimmer of recognition in his eyes.

Being an author is watching an editor remove and juggle around all the carefully placed ;;::,,""!!'s from your manuscript, plus delete all the "u"s from the English spelling of such words as behaviour, honour, etc., that good old Sister Alfreda in your convent-school days spent so much time teaching you to put into your spelling.

Being an author is wearing your book like a scarlet letter that says "I'm Fay, read me!" and rating your friends by the number of copies they buy and circulate.

Being an author is getting a royalty check just as you've broken a tooth on a kernel of popcorn the night before, requiring four trips to the dentist's office at $35 a visit.

Being an author is putting your heart in the hands of your readers.

Being an author is autographing the fly leaf of your book and wishing that, instead of signing your name, you were writing the message of Jesus Christ across the person's heart, soul and spirit.

Being an author is falling to your knees and saying "God, my Father, separate the chaff from the wheat, anoint me with your wisdom and let my work be pleasing in your sight. Use it to touch lives or still my pen—"